J. H Raycroft, Minnie Cron Wheeler, J Young

The progressive art guide

an entirely new method of self-instruction on modern arts, shown in their

progressive stages of completion

J. H Raycroft, Minnie Cron Wheeler, J Young

The progressive art guide
an entirely new method of self-instruction on modern arts, shown in their progressive stages of completion

ISBN/EAN: 9783744739863

Printed in Europe, USA, Canada, Australia, Japan

Cover: Foto ©Suzi / pixelio.de

More available books at **www.hansebooks.com**

THE

✠ Progressive ✤ Art ✤ Guide ✠

(WITHOUT A TEACHER)

An Entirely New Method of Self-Instruction on Modern Arts,
shown in their Progressive Stages of Completion

BY

: : : J. H. RAYCROFT ~ MINNIE CRON WHEELER : : :

ALSO

An Interesting and Instructive Essay

ON THE

INFLUENCE AND HIGHER AIM OF ART

: : : BY J. YOUNG : : :

PROFUSELY ILLUSTRATED

With Large Colored Studies of Flowers and Landscapes, Fac-Similes of Real Oil Paintings,
each of which is accompanied by Outline Drawings, also Numerous Engravings. Full
Size Working Patterns and Designs for New Methods of Needle-Work, in
which all the Stitches used in Making are Illustrated.

J. B. YOUNG & CO., PUBLISHERS
TORONTO, ONT.   ST. JOHN, N.B.
1886.

PREFACE

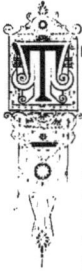

THE reason for the appearance of this book may be said to be three-fold; *First.* The absence of any such work that embraces within its scope, in a plain methodical manner, the progressive stages of Art instructions, commencing at the first principles and carrying the reader forward, step by step, to a degree of perfection. *Second.*—One of the most noticeable and interesting features of our times is the increasing tendency of the people toward the study and practice of the artistic, and the ardent desire expressed by many for a reasonable system of self-instruction. *Third.*—To still further stimulate and encourage that tendency among the people, the fostering of which must have a decided refining effect. These reasons, together with the numerous encouragements we have received, have induced us to undertake the expensive task of publication.

The work is original in its scope and methods of *progressive* instructions; and we congratulate ourselves that we have been able to call to our aid the very best Art specialists in the country. Artists whose paintings and explicit methods of *imparting their knowledge to others* have been received with unbounded favor and delight throughout Canada and the United States. Printed instructions by such prominent Art teachers, given in a progressive plan, cannot but possess nearly every advantage of personal instructions. It may be unnecessary to add that the longer artists labor as specialists in any branch of Art, the more cognizant are they of the difficulties that beset a beginner, and the more mature are their minds and the better qualified are they to impart their instructions. Possibly at no time will their enterprising efforts be more appreciated than at the present time, when the discouragements of wrong methods have been felt by many. We are free to confess that we have no sympathy with those whose practice is to impatiently take the brush from the beginner and do the painting themselves, through a false fear that an imperfect piece of work by a beginner would destroy their reputation as teachers; ignoring the fact that all beginners will produce imperfect work at at the start. Nor are the teachers alone to blame for this pernicious system. Many people are so eager to have a beautiful painting to show friends or parents, that this habit of *teacher-you-do-the-work* system receives encouragement from those who pay for such instructions. Parents have a right and a duty in ascertaining the character of the instructions given their daughters, and insisting that they be taught the rudiments first, and that the progressive stages be mastered one after the other. The existence of mistaken ideas sometimes make it difficult to induce the intending pupil to begin and continue a course of instructions in a proper manner. But a few years have elapsed since the study of "Art" was considered to be suitable and desirable for the wealthy only, and as a means of amusement for idle persons. But now we are pleased to note that these dark days are past and that the morning sun of a new era is upon us, and the masses in general are claiming it as a birth-right that was always intended to be as free as the air, and designed to brighten the homes, increase perceptions of beauties in nature, and refine and cheer the hearts of rich and poor. As a result few homes can be found which have not attained some degree of artistic beauty; and still fewer persons are found who are sufficiently selfish to place an underrated value upon Art work because others of more moderate means are having access to these benefits and pleasures as well as they. It has long been our ambition to supply such a work to the Art-loving people of America, and we trust we have not made a misconception of the tendency of the times, and that to the thousands of homes into which the book may enter, it will bring something of the steadfast-ness of purpose, cheerfulness, and lofty aspirations of the artists.

The work has been explicitly written and carefully executed, and every possible means of descriptive and colored illustrative power has been utilized in order to make it what the title page indicates, a true *"Progressive Art Guide."*   J. B. Y. & Co.

CONTENTS

The Influence and Higher Aim of Art.

paints. The lesson on *solid squares* upon mill board superior to any other in learning the resources and properties of your paints. Copying the shades of different fabrics, stones and rocks excellent subjects for this practice. Table for mixing paints; *proportions* given for all fluis, flowers, landscapes, portraits, and miscellaneous colors. Modifying effects of colors when placed side by side. Complements of colors. How to arrange the colors on the palette. Advantages of such an arrangement. The illustrated "palette key-board." First lesson in painting similar to the first lesson in music, namely, learning the key-board . 26–33

Preliminary Suggestions.

Additional suggestions and encouragements. Special genius not necessary in order to learn painting. Our success in learning depends upon our patience, perseverance, determination, and the earnestness of our desires. John Ruskin's opinion on this subject. The most talented have to study and work, and the patient are always successful. Relative position of the student to the copy. Relative position of the copy to the painting. Management of light. How to study the component parts of a landscape systematically. Position of the "horizon line" in a painting. Peculiarities of mountains. How water is affected by reflection. Peculiarities of trees, graduated sky, and clouds. Graceful lines to indicate the rounded appearance of the ground, etc. Advantages of systematic scrutiny . . 34–38

Canadian Scenes, and How to Paint Them.

BY J. H. BANCROFT.

Diversified views of our own country being received with greater favor than foreign scenes. Our national scenery. Landscapes a favorite with one ..... not so difficult as figure painting. Drawing in outline as a groundwork for painting. ... accompanying outline sketches of the views, and easy methods of transferring them to the canvas. The "pantograph," or how to enlarge *any* picture to *any* size. Free-hand drawing and comparative measurement. How to indicate and lay in the shadows. Detailed instructions for painting "Les Chats Rapids." The beautifully colored study an exact guide in coloring. New discoveries in landscape painting. Explanations of art terms, "high lights," "to warm," "coldness of a tint," "blending," "oiling out," etc. The progressive stages of the painting fully explained. Instructions for mixing and applying paints for each object seen in the study. Finishing touches, etc. 39–48

Instructions for Painting Vancouver View.

The magnificent mountain scenery of British Columbia and the Pacific coast becoming a favorite sketching resort. The charming colored study of "Vancouver View," as seen from the governor's residence, depicts one of the many beautiful mountain scenes that meet the eye in that country. Sketching in or transferring the outlines from the accompanying pencil sketch. Applying the paints for sky, clouds, mountains, rocks, foliage, water, etc. How to represent reflections or shadows as being *under* the water. Another lesson on "the knack of handling the brush." Mounting the colored studies. How to make varnish for the colored & painted studies. How to frame and hang pictures. Additional hints concerning oil paintings and engravings 49–56

° ° ° Contents ° ° °

Moleskin Velvet, or Shadow Painting.

BY MINNIE GION WHEELER.

A decidedly new idea in painting.—But recently introduced into the English art schools.—Remarkable beauty of the work.—Its practical adaptability for the greatest variety of decorative purposes: panels, bracket drapes, strips for sofa cushions, plaques, etc.—Materials. Paints, classified list of brushes, etc.—How to make patterns, and stamp the outlines, from the accompanying sketches.—Tracing the outlines with paint.—How to trim the brushes (*illustrated*).—The names of the different parts of flowers.—Laying in the shadows. Directions for applying paint for the colored study of "Roses, pansies, and calla lilies."—Instructions for the colored study of "Tea roses, Easter lilies, and fuchsias."—Instructions for "Bluebell study."—Instructions for "Pansy study" 57-69

Progressive Art Needle-Work.

Superior advantages of representing the work in progressive stages of completion.—Advantages of having it taught by the aid of *full-sized* working patterns, in which the stitches used in working each design are illustrated.—The *progressive* plan possesses every advantage of personal instructions from the artist.—Reasons why other methods of book instructions have failed.—Their methods failed to show how and where to utilize the stitches, and their patterns were too small to be of practical use.—How to make perforated patterns and do your own stamping.—Stamping with powders.—Recipes for making stamping powder in all colors. New liquid stamping.—French indelible stamping.—Instructions for Scotch thistle design.—Stitches employed in working.—The stem stitch, arrasene stitch, blossom stitch, and foundation stitches, illustrated. Instructions for Dogwood design. Instructions for Red Poppy design, with stitches, illustrated.—Directions for making up Poppy design sofa cushion.—Instructions for Fuchsia design, with stitches used . . . 70-88

vii.

— LIST OF —

Colored Studies, Pencil Sketches, Outline Patterns and Engravings.

The Influence and Higher Aim of Art.

BY J. YOUNG.

HEN properly directed, the influence exercised by the study of Art in the home is probably much greater than at first glance would appear. The grandest and noblest motives that can stir the human heart are frequently those awakened by a thoughtful gaze upon an ideal painting. The kindling of these emotions are the hallowed bonds that unconsciously seem to sustain us and bind us to a higher and nobler nature. We are so situated in our surroundings, and constituted in our natures, that we are continually open to many subtle influences, which help to make or mar us. The various phases of nature, and nature invested by art, with her higher and truer meanings are continually before us, at our meals, during our leisure hours, and when at work, inviting us lovingly to a higher plane of life, and nobleness of character, that nature's God would have us occupy and enjoy. Art, in this connection, acts as a friendly guide to draw us away from the dissipations and deceptions of the world; from the deceit and allurements of our own hearts, to nature's courts and gardens, where we may find subjects for healthful thought, and strength to come back to the bustle of every day life, as giants refreshed with new wine.

Very few persons are so solitarily situated in this country, that visions of unspeakable beauty, messages from a world above matter are denied them;

but the eye must be made clear by observation and culture to enable us to see
the visions, and drink in and assimilate its teachings. But we are glad to know
that the gateways leading to the infinite knowledge, pleasure and beauffes of
the whole universe are open to all, and that the latch-string is always outside
and accessible to the humblest person as well as the highest, and all who will
may enter the artistic and intellectual storehouse, and find treasures of intrinsic
value.   There is truly a land of Havilah open to us, of which it is literally
true, "The gold of that land is good."   Yet, how many of us are cheated out
of the best enjoyments afforded us by these avenues through lack of cultivation of the senses ; or by being too closely occupied with trifles and fashions,
or, perhaps, by thinking that the only source of happiness lies in a heated race for
wealth, and hence, our eyes become dim, our senses numbed, and the avenues
of our thoughts become closed to all those sublimer joys placed within our
reach, and which are the heaven-appointed birthrights of our common humanity.
We have but to surrender ourselves to these friendly elements and place ourselves beneath the radiating influence of art, and all nature is for us. But how
best to assimilate these friendly elements of nature, and benign influences, benefits
and functions of art to our support, refinement, enjoyment and culture, is the
great object.   To this we say, only by observation and properly directed study,
which begins at the first principles, and advances, *naturally and progressively*, from stage to stage ; but not by mere injudicious grinding, which of itself
will produce nothing but dust. If our object is to obtain flour, we must have
wheat first, and *that comes by gradual growth*, but not by grinding. So with
the development of Art knowledge, it must be gradual in its growth and
natural in its development. While we believe that the germ, *or power of growing and developing* our own faculties, exists in a greater or less degree in our
common humanity (some needing only a little sunshine to start the germ
growing, and others perhaps needing sunshine and showers combined), we
would discourage the abuse of those powers through the reversing of the
natural order of things, that is, the *premature grinding process at the start*; but
would encourage the cultivation and development of these faculties in their
natural and scriptural order, "First the seed in the ground, then the blade,

and afterward the full corn in the ear," and lastly comes the grinding. The
study of Art should be undertaken with a view to the furtherance of the
grave purposes of life, with similar objects of purpose as other branches of
education, and not simply as a means of graceful recreation for leisure hours,
but with this great fact ever in view, that *all great arts have for their higher
aim either to contribute to the support of life or its exaltation and enoblement of
character.*

Art influence in the home can only be estimated from the immense
force of its impressions. Its prerogative is, to make those impressions
upon our nature, and give that nature the first direction onward and upward
in the moral channels of all that is good and beautiful. These influences are
indelible and lasting as life, and have a tendency to sweeten the whole cup
of life ; and its restraining and elevating influence is so lasting that it cannot
be easily shaken off; nor, indeed, is its happy recipient anxious to discard such
an agreeable companion, that walks with us in youth, follows us all through
the journey of life, clings to us in death, and fits us for the enjoyment of
the beauties of heaven. From this we may infer the character of *Art influence.* It is like the mighty St. Lawrence, calm and deep, yet moves on in
silent overwhelming power. It is great, silent, irresistible, and lasting, and
amid the most trying storms of life, it infuses a softening spell into our hearts;
even when the cruel world is closing up the sources of sympathy and love.
Who does not feel this influence upon all the diversified habits of life ? The
young hearts are gladdened by it with the hope that they, ere long, will be
enabled to accomplish much that is beautiful. And those in the prime of
life will tell us that many of those reliable principles and noble accomplish-
ments that enrich their souls are those begat b .ie influence of Art in
their earlier days. The aged, as they dote in second infancy, feel its influence, and look with mingled pride and pleasure upon some article of their
own handiwork. It will cling to us like the scent of the poet's vase :

"You may break, you may shatter the vase if you will,
But the scent of the roses will cling round it still."

The influence and study of Art enable us to form some idea, not only of what we are going to be in the world, but also of what we are going to do therein.

Its influence in moulding and developing the individual character along intellectual and moral lines, cannot be easily overestimated:

> "Ingenious Art with her expressive face
> Steps forth to fashion and refine the race."

Oh, beautiful Art! so beneficial in its influence, and that places such glorious possibilities within our reach, what is there not in thee? An able writer has very truthfully said, "It is good not to have been born earlier than the nineteenth century," when we can at least enjoy the dawning influence of Art. But many of us, no doubt, could have rested content until the twenty-first, by which time we have reason to believe that it shall have reached the climax of noonday. Let us hope, however, that with its present onward march this glorious heritage may be ours. And ours it may be, in a degree at least, if we do not content ourselves with a rudimentary knowledge only, or feeding upon husks while a little farther on is a *feast of true bread*. Believing, as we do, that the higher our aims are and the greater our exertions, the more apt are we to reach that "noonday" and bask beneath its radiating and refining influence. The influence of Art, in the hands of really good and clear-headed men, has been made to play an important part in the portrayal of scriptural truth and in the promulgation of religious thought and teachings. The Sabbath-school teacher of an infant class, who is able by a few strokes of the crayon or pencil to convey, through the eye, to the mind *true* conceptions of the teachings of God's Word, possesses superior power of imparting knowledge to his pupils than the one who lacks this power of delineating or disregards the advantages of such an *object lesson* system. And, thus again, the missionary finds that the heathen catches the meaning of his teachings, and believes more readily, when they are pictured out and brought vividly before his eye. While we recognize this powerful and admirable function of Art, we sincerely regret the fact that it has, in the hands of the promoters of false religions, wrought harm, and been made use of, in Christian and heathen lands, in instilling false teachings and wrong conceptions of the Deity.

The surgeon, about to perform an intricate operation, who is able to call to his aid sufficient formative Art-power as will enable him to make a model of that particular portion of the body in putty, or similar substance, and *locate* the arteries in the same, and studies upon this model how he may avoid a possible danger, will, by the aid of such means, materially lessen the dangers, and perform it with assurances of ultimate success. If space permitted, we might enumerate the benefits and influences of Art among all professions and trades, and in all the various walks of life. Many of the most prominent statesmen, distinguished orators, and fluent preachers owe their success largely to their vivid imaginations and remarkable powers of observation and description, which were developed largely during those periods in which they freely used the pencil and the brush.

We observe, also, that ladies who have a knowledge of Art make the best housekeepers. A young lady who has been taught accuracy by a course in drawing and who has had her eyes enlightened by the study and practice of painting, will make her home the richer and better ordered through the advantages of such a training. And if she undertakes the duties of a home in a right spirit she will certainly find use for all she has ever learned. Besides, she will have the aid which habits of order and perseverance, thus learned, will constantly give her.

Can any one estimate the annual loss, to manufacturers and others, caused by defective drawing in patterns and models? Our tradesmen suffer equally as much through lack of such Art knowledge as would enable them to compete more successfully in the markets of the world. Yet, with all its importance, does it not seem strange that the subject receives so little attention in our system of education? The primary object of all Art education should be to aid the individual to support himself in any environment in which he may be placed. But any system of instruction that does not aim at, ultimately, bringing out all the energies of *hand, heart, and head,* is a comparative failure.

One of the most common mistakes of the present day is the failure to utilize
to the fullest extent that which we have learned.   But the higher function of
all true Art is to unfold to us the fullest extent of ascertainable truth concerning visible things, and to reach and develope our finer emotions and
moral feelings.   The artist who addresses his work to the intellect alone,
no matter by what clever sophistries he may defend it, is evidently confining
himself to the lower range of his functions.   Art has no mission to imitate
nature, but has a higher aim and range of meaning; and if it employs con-
ventional terms and commonplace subjects, it does so only as an aid, and
not as an end.   If an exact imitation of nature were all that was desired in
a picture, then an ordinary photograph would possess superior worth to that
of the most brilliant painting.   But the painting is valued pre-eminently
because it has warmth, life, expression, and richness.   It touches the emotions
more than the reality, because it possesses that which the reality has not,
namely, individuality, depth, and suggestiveness.   The true aim is not a servile
imitation of nature, but an investment of natural forms, realities, with a new
and richer meaning, and thus it becomes something more than a mere photographic representation.   Art, in this higher sense of the term, has a meaning,
a purpose of its own, a lesson to teach, a mission to fulfil.   Its mission may be
defined in various ways, but its true aim is always something more than an
appeal to outward sensibilities.   Its mission is to cultivate the higher emotions,
to draw out and develop the nobler and better part of man.

It is fair to judge all phases of Art as we would all forms of books,
namely, by the impressions they give, the lessons they teach, and their
possible future influence on conduct.   With those who believe that life is
something more than a measurement between the cradle and the grave, that
character has a relation to destiny which is not dissolved by death, and that
the results of conduct are carried over beyond the bounds of this earthly existence, no Art, no learning of any sort, can be considered apart from its
moral purpose and results upon character.   It is a fair test of a piece of Art
work to ask, Does it teach purity, goodness and generosity ?   Does it draw
the gazer away from the mere consideration of self ?   Does it carry the mind

into new channels of refining thought, or bring a bit of nature from the fields that furnishes an aid to self-culture? Does it indicate a noble thought, or depict an heroic act? Has it a tendency to refine, to make us nobler and braver? When these are the predominant motives, mistakes and blemishes in execution may well be overlooked and excused; but when these motives are lacking, no grace of expression, no superior touch can atone for them.

Art cannot be admired for Art's sake alone; that is, Art abstracted from its deeper meanings, higher aims, and moral teachings. We must judge a piece of Art work, not so much by the simple quality of its construction, as we would by the suggestions it affords, the emotions it arouses and the lessons it teaches. No painting that does not answer these, or similar questions of motive, purpose, and meaning, is worthy of the appellation of *great, good,* or *beautiful.* And no painting that is impure in its suggestions, or derogatory in its teachings—no matter how near a model of perfection it may be in coloring or execution—is fit to find its way into any home. Another mission true Art is to furnish; high ideals of civilization, advanced examples of nobleness of character, which register the high water mark of civilization. One of the highest things that Art can do, and do successfully, is to set before us a true representation of a noble human being. Much of the march of progress from barbarism to our present state of civilization is due to t' prominence given directly, or indirectly, to the great ideals of character in every age. Especially is this true concerning the Ideal of the Christian religion. Let us not become too desirous of painting life as it is in its fallen or reduced state: but rather to furnish ideals of virtue, beauty, lovliness, and goodness. The words of *Alice Cary* have a forcible application in this direction:

> "You, sir, know
> That you on the canvas are to repeat
> Things that are fairest, things most sweet,—
> Woods and cornfields, and mulberry tree;
> The mother, the lads, with their nest, at her knee.
> But, oh, that look of reproachful woe!
> High as the heavens your name I'll shout
> If you paint me the picture and leave that out."

It is in this direction the force of impressions of true Art, given almost unconsciously, will make itself felt almost resistlessly.   There is no scarcity of pictures of unworthy persons; but how few there are of the truly best men, or their noble actions.   What an important factor would have been contributed to the history of Europe if it had been the object of the people to discern, and of their artists to honor and bear record of the great deeds of their worthiest men, and thus bear record of human acts that invoked God's blessing, and given less prominence to those whose actions were such as deserved His anger.

Had the Greeks given us accurate representations of their great philosophers, or portraits of the heroes of the battles of Marathon and Salamis, or drawings of the battles themselves, they would have rendered us, by such historic pictures, and their country a more signal service than they did by all the vase-paintings, on which the numerous representations of what they fancied to be the figure of the gods are painted.   And so in our own age and country prominence should be given to portraits of really good men and women; persons who have made the country wiser and better for their having lived in it.   The picture of a great man increases our interest in him, and leads us to enquire into the secret of his greatness, or nobleness of character; and as we gaze upon his life-like features upon the canvas, and know something of his life, it would almost seem as though he were speaking to us, encouraging us to follow his virtues, or perchance admonishing us to avoid the errors that prevented him from reaching a higher degree of perfection.   In view of this, does it not behoove the Canadian artist of to-day not only to give to future generations faithful representations of our natural scenery as it now exists, but also to leave upon canvas portraits of the great and good men and women of the present age, as true and salutary indexes of the moral purity of our thoughts, the loftiness of our emotions, and the intellectual state of our minds.

And if the higher aim of Art is to be attained by us, we must study, drink in and assimilate it, so that its nourishment becomes part of our nature, invigorating our life with its inspiration, enjoyments and wisdom.   We must not remain on the outside of the great Milan Cathedral if we would enjoy the grandeur of the picture produced inside by the morning sunlight streaming through the beautiful stained-glass windows. As we go inside what a magnificent sight meets our eyes! So if we would bask in the sunshine of Art, we must direct our steps towards, and endeavor by steady advancement and close application to reach and enter into, its endearing and ennobling shrine. Art must be studied to be fully appreciated. And in view of the increased attention, the marked strides of Art advancement, and the present increasing refining influence upon the hearts of the people, we predict, through the budding of Art, many new joys, happier homes, and purer lives—as Wordsworth says of nature:

—"'Tis her privilege,
Through all the years of this our life, to lead
From joy to joy; for she can so inform
The mind that is within us, so impress
With quietness and beauty, and so feed
With lofty thoughts, that neither evil tongues,
Rash judgments, nor sneers of selfish men,
Nor greetings where no kindness is, nor all
The dreary intercourse of daily life,
Shall e'er prevail against us, or disturb
Our cheerful faith, that all which we behold
Is full of blessings."

Oil Painting.

IN these days there are few persons who are not influenced more or less by the charms of oil paintings. The great variety of subjects, supplied in almost every phase of nature, in flowers, landscapes, animals, portraits, historic scenes, etc., which are capable of the most accurate representation through this medium, all tend to make it a most interesting and fascinating branch of art, and justly commands for it a foremost place. The rapidity with which we are able by this means to convey *through the eye to the mind* the numerous lessons and beauties of nature is one of its greatest charms. Subjects that would take a considerable time to depict in water color can be executed most expeditiously by oil painting, and the most brilliant effects obtained.

There is probably nothing that tends more to the refinement and development of the better nature of men and women than the *study* of nature through art. To a person whose mind has been directed to and follows the higher teachings of art, the beauties of nature will speak to him in a language formerly unknown. The most common things will possess a peculiar charm; the beautiful sunset will no longer pass unnoticed ; the natural woods will furnish food for healthful reflection, and become something more than a mere hunting ground, in which to kill and destroy, in fact a hunter thus influenced will *take more pleasure in studying the merits and habits of a harmless bird*, than in shooting it ; and the heretofore thoughtless youth will take delight in straightening up a partly broken lily, rather than ruthlessly striking it to the ground with his cane. As we prosecute our studies in art, let us endeavor to keep its real benefits, higher teachings and pleasures in view, and remember that the true enjoyment is not to come from a mere perusal of the rudiments of instructions. These are the essential means to an end, *but not the end itself.* And as the first principles, and a thorough knowledge of the various processes of painting is absolutely necessary to its full understanding and complete enjoyment, we will endeavor to furnish a reasonable and easily explained system of instruction, and omit nothing that will aid the youngest beginner, knowing that if the *end* is kept in view, and *the reasons why* certain preliminaries should be carefully studied are given, the reader will be materially encouraged to prosecute his studies patiently and progressively. We will begin by giving and explaining the full

List of Materials for Oil Painting.

PAINTS.

It is necessary at the commencement to have a complete assortment of paints. We do not mean that the reader is to supply himself with the numerous *ready made* tints often recommended by careless dealers ; but have a limited number of *reliable*, well selected colors, and by learning the resources of these paints, by mixing them one's self, we get sufficient variety of tints for any purpose—flowers, landscapes or portraits.

The following classified colors will be found reliable and suitable for all subjects :

WHITES :	YELLOWS:	REDS :
Silver White,	Yellow Ochre,	Vermilion,
or	Light Cadmium,	Light Red,
Flake White.	Medium Cadmium,	Indian Red,
	Orange Cadmium.	Burnt Sienna,
		Madder Lake.

BLUES.	GREENS:	BROWNS and BLACKS:
Permanent Blue,	Terre Verte,	Raw Umber,
Antwerp Blue,	Light Zinober Green.	Bone Brown,
Cobalt Blue.		Vandyke Brown,
		Bitumen,
		Ivory Black.

The cheaper yellows which are used instead of the cadmiums are the chromes, which come in three grades, namely: light, medium and orange; but as these are fugitive colors, and will in time turn black, they are not generally recommended for any painting intended to stand the test of time.

Other colors may be added to the list named, but they are not absolutely necessary, as almost any desired tint may be made by mixing the above named colors. But as different artists have their favorite colors, and their own way of going to work, these will be given with each study, by the artist who painted it.

BRUSHES.

When purchasing brushes for oil paintings, note that there are two kinds used, those made of bristle and those made of red sable. We recommend the *flat* bristle brushes in preference to the round ones. Select brushes in which the bristles are *short*, rather than the long ones. It is a good idea to have a good assortment of brushes. About six or eight flat bristle brushes, from one-eighth to an inch in width. Two or three English or French sable brushes, having flat points, numbers 5, 8, and 11, will be needed. It is not necessary to buy a special blender, as a clean, dry, flat bristle brush will answer for all the blending of the skies and dragging together of the edges of tones that are necessary.

PALETTE, EASEL, AND MAHL STICK.

A good size palette should be selected, so as to have plenty of room to mix the paints, and keep each plat apart from the others. The palette should be from eight to ten inches in width at its narrowest part, and about sixteen inches in length. Obtain one that is *unvarnished*, made of cedar, (or similar wood) and of oval shape. Before using, it should be well oiled with linseed or poppy oil, applying the oil thickly and letting it soak into the wood.

The easel may be cheap, or as elaborate as suits the reader's purse. One for ordinary use may be made from three straight bars of pine wood, of about six feet in length; each bar being one and a half inches wide by three-fourths of an inch thick. A number of holes are made at equal distances in two of the bars. These two bars are then securely fastened at the top. The third bar is also attached at the top, by means of a hinge, which permits the easel to be raised or lowered as desired. Two wooden pegs to hold the painting in place upon the easel, complete this necessary article. (See illustration of easel in chapter "Preliminary Suggestions.")

The mahl stick is used to steady the hand while painting. It, as well as the palette, is held in the left hand, while the knob is rested against the painting, thus affording a good support to the right hand while painting. It is not an absolute necessity to the list of materials, as one of the brushes held in the left hand in the same manner will in most cases answer equally as well.

The other articles necessary may be summed up briefly: a bottle of Soehnee's French Retouching Varnish, a few sticks of charcoal for sketching in the outlines, a bottle of linseed or poppy oil, a bottle of refined spirits of turpentine, and a

PALETTE KNIFE.

This is used for mixing paints before they are applied to the canvas. It is also used in applying paint to represent objects requiring a thick application of paint, such as stone, mason-work, rocks, rough, rocky roads, etc. The application of paints with a palette knife should not, however, be attempted by a novice until he has had considerable experience with the brush. It may not be amiss to mention the use of

REFINED SPIRITS OF TURPENTINE.

It is simply mixed with the paints for the *first* coating, only to make them dry quickly, and to clean the brushes while painting.

SICCATIVE DE COURTRAY AND SICCATIVE DE HARLEM.

These are drying preparations (either of which may be used), which when mixed with the paints, cause them to dry quickly. "Siccative de Harlem" is mixed in *equal parts* with boiled linseed oil, or poppy oil. Either of these preparations are good, but "Siccative de Courtray" is a favorite with many, and should be used in the proportion of *one* drop of siccative to *five* of oil. Be careful not to use too much siccative, as the painting is apt to crack if dried too quickly. It should *always* be mixed with oil, when one wishes to finish up a picture rapidly ; but when each coating of paint is given plenty of time to dry before resuming work, poppy oil is sufficient without the siccative.

VARNISHING PAINTINGS.

It is generally known that a painting should not be permanently varnished until it has been painted a year or so ; but as the paints become dull when dry, a temporary varnish called "Soehnee's French Retouching Varnish," is applied, which brings the colors back to their former brilliancy, and will last a a year or so, when the painting may be given another coating without doing it an injury.

Before varnishing a picture, be careful to remove all dust, and wipe it well with a thoroughly-damped, clean, soft cloth ; as soon as it drys, lay the painting *flat* upon a low table. Now dip a large *flat* bristle brush into the saucer containing the varnish, and pass it back and forth over the painting in long sweeps, commencing at the top, and work towards the bottom. This must be done quickly, as the varnish dries very rapidly ; and must be done carefully, so that no spots are left uncovered, as it is necessary to completely cover it as you go. One can ascertain if there be any parts not covered by holding the painting up to the light frequently while applying the varnish ; should such occur, *immediately* pass a brush, full of varnish, over the part before proceeding with the rest. Do not be alarmed if a froth, or bluish mist, shows on the painting when varnishing, as this will disappear when dry,

CANVAS, MILL BOARDS, ACADEMY BOARDS, ETC.

Of late years there has been such an increase of materials upon which to paint, that we will not attempt to enumerate them all, but be content with noting a few of them, and offer a few brief suggestions regarding them that may be profitable to the new beginner. Again we say, *get good materials* in selecting your canvas, etc. With good tools and good materials you can do good, lasting work. It is a clear case of "false economy" to use cheap cotton canvas for a painting of any importance. Get that made of linen, as the cheaper kind made of cotton will shrink in time and crack the painting. The canvases manufactured by Windsor & Newton are among the best made, and may be bought by the yard, or stretched in wooden frames, of different sizes. This comes in four different varieties, viz.: *the single primed, the smooth finish, the twilled,* and *the Roman canvas.* The last named is very coarse in texture. It is purely a matter of taste as to which is chosen. But the single primed is a good canvas for all kinds of painting, and is kept by all dealers, and may be painted upon without any more preparation, although some artists further prepare it by painting it thickly all over with a light gray tint. When this is done it must be allowed to dry quite hard; it is then scraped with the palette knife, so as to remove all roughness; this done, take a large flat bristle brush and give it a thorough application of oil *(in other words, "oil it out")* before painting over such a surface.

The other materials upon which to paint are: Ebonized wood, wooden panels, mill boards, academy boards, etc. Academy boards are better adapted for small easel paintings and decorated cards. They are thiner and cheaper than the mill boards, but should not be used in the large sizes, as they will warp. They can be purchased in different sizes, from 18 x 24 down to 6 x 9 inches, which cost but ten cents each; the large sizes are cheaper accordingly, and can be cut to any desired size.

The mill boards make a firm foundation for a painting of medium size; and where a fine finish is desired, they are often selected instead of canvas. They come in about the same sizes as the academy boards, and furnish a

foundation equally as firm as wood, and will not warp.   They also possess a
fine smooth surface upon which to paint.   But for large paintings, the canvas
is always used.   When possible procure the canvas ready stretched upon
wooden frames of different sizes, as the cost is moderate.

But for the benefit of those who may live a distance from towns and
cities, and find it sometimes difficult to procure the canvas in frames of the
si. wanted, we will endeavor to explain the method of stretching, and describe
how to make that simple little article called

THE CANVAS FRAME OR STRETCHER.

Those who buy canvas by the yard must necessarily cut it, and have the
stretcher made to correspond with the size and shape desired for the painting.
Procure four bars of pine wood, measuring an inch and a half in width by
three-quarters of an inch in thickness.   The length of the bars of course
depend upon the size of the subject to be painted.   The upper side of the
bars over which the canvas is stretched should be planed perfectly smooth,
and slightly beveled towards the inside.   They are then mortised together, in
the same way as a slate frame, and are made oblong or square, as desired.
The mortises are to be made so as to fit neatly, as no pegs or glue must be used.
Four small wooden wedges to be used in tightening up the canvas after it has
been tacked upon the stretcher, will complete the frame.   Now cut the canvas
three-fourths of an inch larger *all around* than the stretcher, so that the canvas
will be large enough to permit it to be tacked to the *outside* edges of the
stretcher.   The canvas is attached to the stretcher in the following manner :
Place the stretcher upon the canvas, leaving a margin of equal width all around.
Now catch the canvas in the middle of one end, and turn it over the outside
edge of the stretcher, and drive a tack there ; then take a pair of pincers and
catch the canvas in the middle of the end opposite, drawing the canvas
tightly ; insert another tack.   Next, put a tack in the middle of *each side*,
always tacking the canvas to the *outside* edge of the stretcher, and *not* on
the *flat* side.   Be sure that you get the canvas on evenly — not pulled
crooked or bias—before going further.   If such should occur, carefully draw

out the tack (using a chisel), and straighten before proceeding further. Now drive tacks at the corners and middle distances, using the pincers to draw the canvas over the outside edge of the stretcher, *each* time a tack is inserted, and then put the tacks an inch and a half apart all round. You now insert one of the wooden wedges (mentioned above) at the *four inside* corners of the stretcher. A slight stroke of the hammer on each of these will spring the joints apart and stretch the canvas to its full limit. This is called *keying up the canvas*, and is quite necessary to remove wrinkles.

PREPARING CANVAS FROM ORDINARY UNBLEACHED LINEN.

There are numerous ways of preparing canvas for painting in oil, but most people prefer that which comes ready prepared by experienced manufacturers, as paintings executed upon such canvas will not crack or peel off, and can be had in different shades. Some of our readers, living at a distance from art stores, may wish to prepare their own canvas from linen, and thus economize in this direction. The method usually adopted is as follows: Procure a piece of good, strong, unbleached linen, the desired size, and see that it is evenly woven; the edges should be hemmed to prevent fraying out. It is then fastened to the stretcher, in the manner described in the foregoing paragraph. Key it up sufficient to tighten it fairly well. You now make a preparation of thin liquid glue, and spread it all over the linen, as evenly as possible. This must be allowed to dry thoroughly, when you then give it a coating of light gray paint, made by mixing silver white and a little ivory black, made quite thin by adding turpentine. This makes what is called the *single primed* canvas, and is preferred by many without any further preparation, and furnishes a very agreeable surface upon which to paint, the threads of the linen showing through. The *smooth-finish* canvas is the result of still another coat of paint, thinned this time with linseed oil instead of turpentine.

How to Mix and Arrange the Palette.

THE problem of combining different colors in order to produce a desired tint, and know just how much of each color to use, is perhaps one of the most formidable difficulties that meets the new beginner. It will be found, however, with a little properly directed study and practice, not to be so difficult as would first appear.

Strictly speaking, there are but three colors in nature, these are *red, yellow,* and *blue.* These are known as the "Three Primaries." Orange, green, purple, and all other tints, are simply composed from these primaries. When regarding a color in nature, or in a colored study, if it be not one of the primaries, the reader has then to consider in what degree it is composed of them. For instance, if orange is the color under consideration, the proper quantities of red and yellow must be determined by mixing a little of each, and then adding a little of one or the other, until the desired shade of orange is obtained. If green is desired, mix the yellow and blue together, adding a very little red, to subdue the brilliancy of the green; thus, again, with purple, which is made by mixing red and blue, the addition of a little yellow destroys its purity. In the case of orange, a little blue mixed with the red and yellow will subdue its brilliancy. It is impossible to say just how much of each paint is to be used, as this will depend upon the tint desired. The reader must learn by practice, how to mix paints in their proper proportion, and it will soon become almost a matter of instinct, to feel just what color is needed to produce a certain tint, or to counteract too much of something else.

It is a good practice for a beginner to experiment, and see how many different tints he can make, out of the paints he has at hand, and thus discover their properties, and learn their combinations. For instance, take a piece of mill board, rule it off into numerous equal squares. Commence with the pure paints, as they come from the tubes, taking Antwerp blue, light cadmium, and white ; and by mixing them in *different proportions*, see how many different shades of green you can make, and fill a square with each shade.

Now take madder lake, cobalt blue, and white, and see how many different tints of purple and violet you can make, in another row of squares.

It will be apparent (even to the untrained eye) that the different colors, as seen in the various squares, lack something ; although they look quite pretty, and we feel that *something more* is needed, to give the green the proper quality. So we again mix Antwerp blue, light cadmium, and white ; *but this time we add a little ivory black, and vermilion,* and notice that the greens lose their crudeness, and we have before us the right shade of green to represent the greens seen in leaves and foliage. Now mark off some more squares, and by mixing these *five* colors, varying their proportions, see how many shades of green can be made. It will prove interesting to compare these shades with those squares of green having no black or vermilion in them. This is the way all colors are mixed for painting ; but do not mix them too much ; just enough to make them combine nicely, as too much mixing has a tendency to make the tints dull. Remember, also, that no color is used alone (except in moleskin velvet painting), but must be mixed with those that have a qualifying effect. A little ivory black may be safely used with everything ; and white is almost always mixed with other paints, sometimes in *very* small quantities.

Another practice, in mixing paints, is, to place different materials of cloth beside the easel, and copy the shades on mill board. It will require a little experimenting, mixing one color with another, and adding a little of this and a little of that. This is an excellent practice for a beginner. A collection of small stones of different colors, pieces of rock, are also desirable subjects for this practice. We append a table for mixing paints, from which the reader may gain some points of value.

Miscellaneous Colors.	PARTS.					
	Ivory Black.	Emerald Green.	Prussian Blue.	Vermilion.	Light Cadmium or Yellow.	White.
Brown	3			2		
Green			1		1	
Purple			2	3		
Crimson	1			8		
Vermilion				15	1	
Lavender			3	1		8
Buff					3	1
Straw					1	1
Fire				1	2	
Gold					5	1
Silver, Steel, or Glass	1					10
Marble			1			20
Black	2			1		
Clear White			1			50
Portrait Colors.						
Flesh Color			1	5	1	50
Sallow Color				5	1	50
Lips and Cheeks				1		1
White of Eyes			1			10
Hair.						
Black	2			1		
Golden	1				5	3
Light					1	3
Auburn	1			3		
Grey	1					3
Brown	1			1	4	
Eyes.						
Black (Iris, Brown) Pupil Black						
Hazel		1		1	4	
Blue			1			4
Grey	1					5
Brown	1				3	
Landscape.						
Deep Foliage		3	1			
Light Foliage		3			1	
River Water			2			6
Ocean Water			2		1	6
Sky at Noonday			1			1
Sunset			2	1		2
Mahogany	1			8		
Oak					2	1

*For Portraits, Blue Black, Light Red, Rose Madder and Yellow Ochre are all used, proportioning them as best suits the subject.

MODIFYING EFFECT OF TINTS, WHEN PLACED SIDE BY SIDE.

It would be well for the reader, at this juncture, to note how different colors modify each other by being placed close to, or side by side with another. It will be found, for instance, that a dull grey will look much more blue than was expected when a bright orange is put beside it.   A dull color will look still more dull, and a bright color increased apparently in brilliancy, if the two be brought together.   It is by experience only that we learn how to take advantage of this, or to avoid it when the effect is not wanted.   This harmony is, moreover, a study of great importance to the amateur, and may be pursued with interest by all, as it is common to all kinds of painting.

Complementary colors generally agree well together, whether placed side by side, or round about as in backgrounds, when one of them is darker or deeper in tone than its neighbor.

Here we give a list of these colors according to the natural order of the solar spectrum :

> The complement of red is green.
> The complement of yellow is violet.
> The complement of blue is orange.
> The complement of violet is lemon yellow.
> The complement of orange is blue.
> The complement of green is red.
> The complement of indigo is ochre.
> The complement of black is white.

To the artist the word *complementary* signifies that if you place, for example, some red on white ground, that red produces on the eye an influence which casts a green tinge on all that surrounds it, or that is in its immediate vicinity ; and, *vice versa*, green throws a red tinge.   Red has a greater intensity by its neighborhood to green, and green is strengthened in brilliancy by being near red.

The more luminous the colors are the more this contrast of complementaries is perceptible. By experimenting on each one of the simple colors in the above list, one will easily comprehend it. Two bands colored with two complementary colors, placed side by side and looked at in the sun, almost hurt the eye at the line of their contiguity.

It is well to place colors on different backgrounds. It will be seen that black grounds lighten the colors placed on them, and that white grounds, on the contrary, give them more force, or darken them by heightening the value of their tone. All paintings on white grounds should be executed rather pale, in order to avoid harshness.

By following up these experiments, the following inferences will be confirmed: Carmines go well with water-green; sky blue always goes well with pale orange; dark blue with deep orange; turquoise with violet blue. Purple, which partakes of blue, goes well with warm ochreous shades and yellow. Greys go well with every color.

HOW TO ARRANGE THE PALETTE FOR OIL PAINTING.

This important item in painting, is very similar to one's first lesson in music, namely, that of learning the key-board of the piano, which must be thoroughly mastered before one can hope to play finished tunes. So with painting, we must learn to arrange our palette in convenient form and regular order, so that we will readily know the place of each paint, almost without looking; and so as to have only those colors on our palette—key-board—that are really necesssary, and which, with their combinations, are used in the subject we are about to paint. This method has many advantages. It spreads out before the eye the greatest variety of tints, ranging from one end of the chromatic scale to the other, thus enabling one to *see* just what shades to select in order to produce any desired tint. This plan will be found to make the mixing of paints a matter of very plain sailing indeed, as well as greatly increase our rapidity in painting. Procure a large, oval palette, which should be well oiled with linseed oil, and when dry, begin

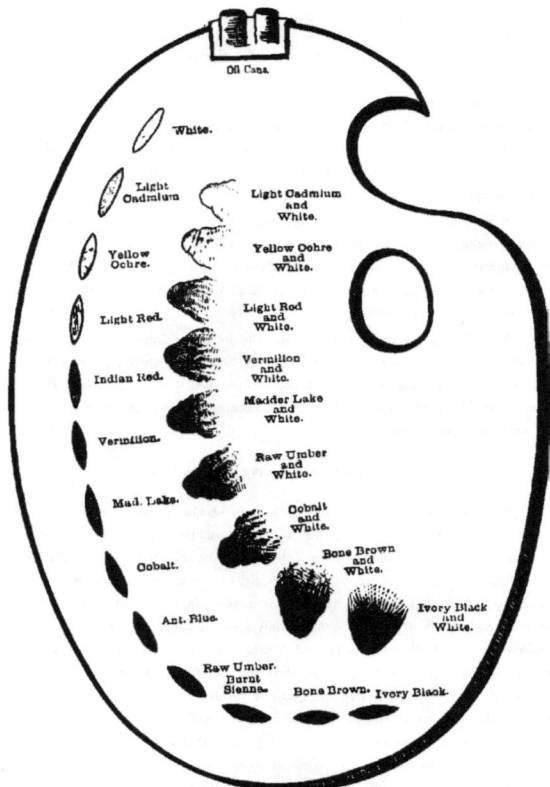

PALLET KEY BOARD.

arranging the paints in the following manner:— Take the tube containing silver white, and press out what seems sufficient white for the painting under consideration, and place it at the upper end of the palette, an inch from the outside edge. Now put yellow ochre, an inch and a quarter below the white, then in the following order, place light red, vermilion, madder lake, cobalt, Antwerp blue, raw umber, burnt sienna, bone brown, and ivory black, leaving about an inch and a quarter between each plat of paint. This is known as the regular palette. If other colors are wanted, place them with the class of paints to which they belong, and between the plats. For instance, if light-cadmium is to be used, we know that it belongs to the *yellow class;* hence we place it just above the yellow ochre. Again, if Indian red is needed, we place it below the light red; permanent blue, zinober green, and terra verte, are placed in the same relation, to cobalt and Antwerp blue.

Just before you commence painting, another inside row of paints is arranged, beginning exactly opposite the yellow ochre. A little yellow ochre is then taken from the first row and placed, as the first paint, in the second row, then a little white is taken (using a palette knife) from the first row, and mixed loosely with the yellow ochre; thus forming a variety of shades of yellow, from pure yellow ochre, down to white. Now mix light red with white in the same manner; vermilion and white is then mixed, forming different shades of pink; then comes madder lake and white, raw umber and white, cobalt and white, ivory black and white. The engraving "Palette Key-Board," plainly illustrates the correct arrangement. By this plan the paints are kept clean, as the greater portion of the painting is done from the second row; thus leaving the pure colors of the first row to be used only when pure touches are wanted. After the day's work is finished, only the row of paints in which white has been mixed need be removed. The outside row of pure paints are left on the palette, as they will keep fresh enough for the next day, when one can add a little fresh paint to each plat where needed, or add a little oil, should they become dry.

Preliminary Suggestions.

AS we enter upon the subject of applying color, it may be of service to some of our readers, who may decide to practise from these instructions, to receive a few additional suggestions and encouragements.

First, we deem it not out of place to say a few words concerning, what we believe to be, a common mistake among people in general, namely, those oft-repeated assertions: "I have no taste for painting," or, "I have no *genius* for things of that sort. I must be *born* with a natural talent before I can hope to succeed." It does seem a little singular that we never stop to reason, in this direction, with regard to writing, arithmetic, grammar or any other subject. Nor would such an excuse, were it pleaded ever so earnestly, be considered a valid reason why we should excuse ourselves from such studies. But we strike right in and master the first principles of each; and ere long we have the gratifying assurances that *our talents*, or genius, grow, and are being generated by our own efforts. It is in the degree that we apply ourselves, and the manner in which we concentrate our study, and in proportion to the amount of determination we evince in our efforts, that we succeed in cultivating a *genius*. I am bold to say, that three-fourths of the so-called "natural genius" we see in those who have excelled in their various vocations, is that created by themselves, by hard, well-directed work, close application, constant use, and reserving the knowledge they thus gain, by their *own untiring efforts*. We are free to admit, that some learn more readily than others; but there are numerous examples to show that *patience perseverance* and *determination*, has succeeded in the end, in a more eminent degree, than those who learned more readily, but lacked these *three* necessary elements of success. The words of that eminent artist, John Ruskin, carry forcible weight in this connection, when he says, "But I shall be able to show you, without doubt, in the course of our studies that the achievements of art which have been usually looked upon as the result of peculiar inspiration, have been arrived at only through long courses of wisely directed labor, and under the influence of feelings which are common to all humanity."

If, therefore, the reader has the courage to begin, and persevere with the determination that nothing will discourage him, and master and apply certain leading principles, he will find that no wonderful *genius* is required in order to succeed beyond an earnest desire. And he will find, too, that the application of these leading principles will render the study of painting not so difficult as expected. It is encouraging to know that the most talented have to work and study, and that the patient are always successful.

Need we go to the field of music to discover that the same rule holds good to a large degree. Shall we ask that clever musician, "How in the world did you become such a fine player?" She would most likely answer, "By learning the rudiments first, and then following this up with vigorous, energetic study and continued practice." Or probably she would answer as did the old musician with a harp, when asked the same question, "By being at it, and always at it." Those who find difficulty in learning the rudiments of painting should encourage themselves by the remembrance that many of our greatest literary men gave but poor evidence of success at the commencement of their course. When we know that one of the finest poems that adorns the English language ("Gray's Elegy"), occupied a number of years in its production, and was written bit by bit, pruned and re-pruned, until it stands out as *the* perfect gem of poetical composition, we are led to believe that the untiring energy, patience, and determination of the author had more to do in making that poem the grand success that it is, than the so-called "Natural Genius" that was born in him. The writer is a firm believer in the doctrine (as applied to Art), "That what man *has done*, man *can do*," if he will put himself through the same discipline, the same study, make the same determined effort, and have the same ardent desire (conditions of health being equal), and that, "Where there is a will there is a way", and that painting is not an exception to these rules. The reader will find that the hand, which but an instrument of the mind, with a little practice, will become obedient to the *will*. Of course there will be difficulties, but these, instead of discouraging us, should stimulate us to greater effort, knowing that every difficulty we *meet* and *overcome*, are but sign-boards that tell us we are on the road to success. And when mastered, one after the other, cannot but be factors that contribute to our enjoyment of the victories thus gained. On the other hand, if *no* difficulties present themselves, the reason is apt to be, that we have given the subject such a half-hearted study as not to discover them; and, naturally enough, when no difficulties arise, no new discoveries are made; hence our energies lag, and our interest becomes less, and we begin a retreat, instead of making steady advancement. Let us start out on the right road to Art knowledge, and follow that path with unremitting vigor, and happy success will ultimately crown our efforts.

POSITION OF THE STUDENT AND COPY WHILE PAINTING.

Seat yourself (or stand) directly in front of your easel, so that a direct line, if drawn from your eye, would strike the centre of the mill board or canvas upon which you are about to paint, and place the object you copy just above the mill board (see illustration.) or on a low stool just below it, giving it a slant of about *three* inches to the foot. This can be done by placing a book on its edge, *under* the upper edge of your copy. The object of this is to enable you to look at your copy (*in the centre also*) without having to raise or lower your head.

Position of Copy while Painting.

Sit in an upright position. There is no need of stooping over your work; it is bad for the health, and does not contribute to the free handling of the brush. Always use the easel in painting, as it is impossible to evince freedom in your work when in a cramped position.

MANAGEMENT OF LIGHT.

This is an important item in painting, and should receive careful attention. A north light is to be preferred, when possible, as it is steadier, and less affected by the direct rays of the sun. If there are other windows in the room they should be darkened, so as to admit light from one window only. The window at which you are about to paint should have the lower part curtained off, so as to let the light come in from the top. Now place your easel in front of the window, and seat yourself in front of the easel, so that the light will strike your copy and canvas over your left shoulder. You must arrange the light so that it will not be too strong, as this is apt to lead to coarse coloring. On the other hand, you must avoid a dull light, as this has a contrary effect. Before beginning to draw in the outlines of the studies, it is well to

STUDY THE LANDSCAPES SYSTEMATICALLY.

Observe that the "Horizon Line" (which marks the termination of the land with the sky) should never be exactly in the middle of a picture, as a painting is considered bad in composition, when divided into two equal parts. You can usually keep the painting as high, or as low as you wish; but, as a rule, at least one-third of the entire space occupied by the painting, should be left for the sky. Notice, also, that in all well executed studies, or paintings, where there is land, water, and sky, that these *three* divisions are *not* equally divided. Now notice the wavy appearance of the mountains, and how the light is focused upon their tops; and how they repeat each other's form, in singular regularity. *(See Study of "Vancouver Views.")*

Next, look at the water, and observe how it is effected by reflections of green trees, pink sky, mountains, etc. Examine the trees, notice that they generally incline a little one way or the other (owing, sometimes, to their position on sides of rocks, or prevailing winds), and that one side of the tree usually shows the branches a little heavier than the other. Notice, also, that the sky is not one even mass of color but is *always graduated* in at least two directions, namely, from the upper portion downwards, and from side to side; and one corner is darker than the other. The sky opposite the sun is darker than the rest, on the *same* level.

Now gaze a moment at the clouds. The highest ones seem perfectly still, and in groups; while the *middle* and lower clouds seem to float in the air, and are more distinct in shape. Notice their pleasing forms against the dark sky. In examining the ground, notice that it is never *flat*, but shows a series of rounded or angular forms, more or less broken, and these can be indicated by graceful lines.

The study of this paragraph will give the reader a clearer idea of the different parts that go to make up his copy, and aid him materially in sketching it in outline, before painting. It will also prove of infinite value, when he begins sketching from nature. It will also help us to appreciate the work of more advanced painters, in whose work these and other points have been systematically observed.

Canadian Scenes and How to Paint Them.

By J. H. RAYCROFT.

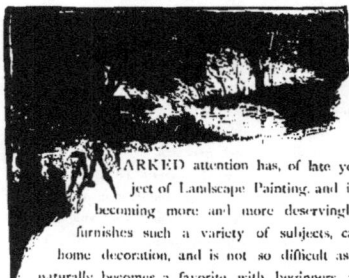

MARKED attention has, of late years, been given to the subject of Landscape Painting, and is still growing in favor, and becoming more and more deservingly appreciated. And as it furnishes such a variety of subjects, capable of being utilized in home decoration, and is not so difficult as "Figure Painting," it very naturally becomes a favorite with beginners and amateurs. Everything that can charm the eye, warm the heart, and increase our love and appreciation of nature—and nature's God - is to be found associated with landscapes. In the wide range of the world's scenery, that occupies the attention of the artist, few places can be more interesting to Canadians and Americans, than the diversified views of our own country. Especially is this true, as he beholds the grandeur of form and color of the snow-capped Rocky Mountains, as seen in British Columbia, and the magnificent variety of the Rideau, Ottawa, and St. Lawrence. Scenes that embrace, in their composition, the most brilliant and gorgeous tints, ranging from one end of the chromatic scale to the other.

Who has not heard of the "Les Chats Rapids," with its beautiful foliage, lovely hills, and dashing waterfalls. Surely the words "Canadian Scenes," must have a pleasant sound to Canadians; for therein is included everything that is truly picturesque, much that should awaken our interest, call out our gratitude to the Giver of all beauty, and cause us to feel proud of our National Scenery. And yet all this goodness and munificence is a dead letter to many of us, through lack of culture of the senses by which these gifts are enjoyed. There is much in nature that we do not half enjoy, and if we will but *open* our minds to the study and enjoyment of art, we may find tranquil pleasure spread about on every side, and will soon become more *sensible* and *susceptible* to the beauties of nature, which will speak to us in a language unknown to those who are less refined, and not so easily impressed. The cultivation of an artistic, nature-loving mind is one of the most edifying, as well as useful, privileges that our Creator has placed within our reach. We must have more knowledge, to enable us to enjoy the beauties of nature and art.

A personal visit, by the lover of art, to the many points of natural beauty and interest, throughout the Dominion, would doubtless quicken his perceptions of beauty, and expand his artistic mind. As he gazes on the lofty mountain peaks, and watches the swift-flying clouds break against their craggy sides, or listens to the song of the turbulent rapids, or views, with studious intent, the brilliant sunset, he must feel that he is enjoying a treat, that would be appreciated by all lovers of the sublime. While in other localities, quiet, pretty views will meet the eye, possessing beauties of a calm and rural kind.

It is of course desirable, before beginning any kind of painting, to have as a foundation, a fair knowledge of drawing; as the brush is *not* the correct medium with which to learn to draw. The necessity of proper sketching will be apparent to all; for when the outlines are correctly drawn in, one is enabled to devote the entire attention to painting, and have the assurance that when it is completed, it is not rendered useless by faulty drawing, which cannot be hid by the best "brush execution." How 'en do we see paintings in which are evidences of considerable skill in coloring, etc., rendered useless on account of careless drawing. But as no very difficult effect is attempted, we think, that to paint any of the studies by the aid of the accompanying sketches, will be readily accomplished by any one.

After studying, *systematically*, the various points of the view, "Les Chats Rapids," as suggested in the last chapter, begin by

TRANSFERRING OR SKETCHING THE OUTLINES.

To do this accurately, is a matter of great importance, as the beauty of the finished picture depends largely upon this. And with a view to accuracy, an outline sketch is given with each study, from which the leading lines may be transferred directly to the mill board, or canvas, in the following manner: Procure some powdered charcoal, and with a soft rag, rub it all over the back of the accompanying outline sketch. Shake off the surplus powder, enough will remain to make the outlines. Now place this sketch upon the mill board or canvas, *powdered side* facing the mill board, being careful to secure the sketch *firmly* to the mill board, by means of small tacks, or otherwise. Now go over the outlines with a tracing point, or hard pencil. Carefully remove the sketch, and you have all the leading lines of the study, accurately sketched upon the material. But as this will rub off, we now take a little burnt sienna, and ivory black, and turpentine, mixed quite thin, and with a small round camel's hair brush, go over the outlines carefully. This is a rapid and excellent method, especially for those who are deficient in free hand drawing.

If the reader does not wish to soil the outline sketches that accompany the studies, *another piece* of thin paper may be rubbed with the powder, and *this* sheet placed upon the material to be painted, and the outline sketch placed upon it, and traced in the manner described.

Should the reader desire, at any time, to paint upon a dark material, on which the charcoal would not show, he may rub red pastel, or crayon, on the back of the sketch, instead of charcoal. It will be seen that any flat copy may, by this means, be transferred in correct outlines to the material to be painted. Such an easy method is preferred by many, who do not aim at perfecting themselves in art.

THE PANTOGRAPH

Is another simple and accurate device, by means of 'which the outlines of any design, *landscapes, figures,* or *flowers,* may be readily obtained. It is a small wooden, frame-like instrument (costing about forty cents), having a tracing peg attached in one part, and a pencil, or stick of charcoal, is placed at the right-hand side, arranged so that all the operator has to do, is to follow the outlines of the study with the tracing peg, and the pencil to his right will make the exact markings on the material. By this simple instrument, the outlines of any design may be reproduced, the exact size or *enlarged to any size at one operation.* But those whose aim it is to become artists, will sketch their subjects from the colored studies, and from nature, by

FREE HAND DRAWING AND COMPARATIVE MEASUREMENT.

This is done by drawing a few leading lines first (such as the water line, at the base of the trees, near the foot of the mountain, and at the base of those trees seen in the middle distance ; then locate the points where the water breaks to form the falls, and the water line at the base of the falls), and then selecting some object, such as one of the trees in the middle distance, draw this tree in first, and make this your standard, when drawing in any portion of the study. Compare *every* object in the distance with this tree, and determine, by your eye, whether they are half as high, or less than half as high, or more than half as high. Thus again, compare all objects in the foreground, with this same standard, and see whether they are once, twice, or three the size of your standard. In this way, the *trunks* of trees, widths and heights of different objects are compared, and the scale of distance is established, by the relative proportions of such objects. Notice how much smaller the trees in the distance appear, when compared with those in the foreground, though in reality they may be the same size. The outlines and general proportions are sketched in first with a stick of charcoal sharpened to a point. Should mistakes occur, the charcoal can be rubbed off with a clean rag. This done, go over the charcoal outlines with a thin mixture of burnt sienna, ivory black, and turpentine, using a small camel's hair brush, and make the outlines light. Then outline the general form of the clouds, and also the form of the shadows, where they meet the lights, as seen in the water of this study, dividing them into simple masses. This done, the next step is to

INDICATE THE SHADOWS.

This is done by applying, with a flat bristle brush, a tone made by mixing burnt sienna and ivory black; made very thin and light by mixing in plenty of turpentine, and filling in the shadows with a flat even tone. Make no effort to put in any details, reflections, or half tints, but simply block them in, leaving a simple effect of light and shade. When the outlines are finished, and shadows located, the reader is enabled to give undivided attention to the painting. If it be found, on examination, that the burnt sienna and ivory black has been applied to the wrong place, it can be completely removed by dipping a rag into pure turpentine and placing it over the finger and rubbing it over the spot.

INSTRUCTIONS FOR APPLYING THE PAINT FOR " LES CHATS RAPIDS."

This beautiful scene is most faithfully represented in its natural beauty, and furnishes an excellent study for painting in oil, or water-color. It combines all the leading lessons that are embodied in any landscape, namely : Variegated clouds, mountains, rocks, and beautiful foliage, having this peculiar advantage, that it furnishes a lesson on *extremely rough* as well as *gently flowing* water, as seen in the foreground. It is not, however, a difficult study, and if the reader has followed the preceding suggestions, and has the outlines accurately traced upon the material, it will be found an easy matter to paint it, especially when we have such a perfect representation of a real painting in oil for our guide in coloring. The reader is thus enabled to mix the paints, adding a little of one or the other, and then compare with the color seen in the study.

Beginners are apt to aim at over-finish, and extreme smoothness, irrespective of consistent results. These points in landscape painting are, fortunately, coming into disfavor; while those which evince free handling of the brush, breadth, and simplicity of treatment, are considered artistic. An important item towards gaining this object is, by using *good sized brushes* at the start. Having, by *any* of the methods described, gotten the outlines correctly traced, or drawn upon your canvas or mill board, begin by arranging the palette similar to the method already described (see illustration, " Palette-Key-Board " P. 31); but place *only* such colors on your palette as are used in this study, which are as follows : Silver white (or flake white), Naples yellow, yellow ochre, light red, rose madder, vermilion, cobalt blue, light zinober green, terre verte, burnt sienna, raw umber, Vandyke brown, bone brown, bitumen, and ivory black. These colors are all arranged as the outside row of the palette ; and when the reader is directed to mix any of these paints, it is understood he is to take a palette knife, and lift a *portion* of paint from one of these plats, and place it a little nearer the centre of the palette, and then mix it with others to obtain the desired tint ; and thus leave the outside row of paints perfectly pure, to be resorted to at any time. You now place the mill board upon the easel and begin painting. The sky is always painted first, commencing at the upper part and working downwards.

Take some silver white from the first row of paints, and place it opposite the plat of yellow ochre ; you now mix a little yellow ochre with this silver white ; mix in thoroughly, just enough of yellow ochre to give it a pale creamy tint, using the palette knife for mixing. We will, for sake of convenience, call *this* mixture *prepared white.*

We see by the colored study, that we have *three* distinct shades of blue in the sky ; we must, therefore, mix three different tints of blue to correspond with these, and place them in *separate* plats, upon our palette, in the second row. For the *darkest* shade, take a small quantity of *prepared white,* to this add a little cobalt blue, a *very* little ivory black, and rose madder to warm. (" To warm " means to lessen the cold bluish tendency of a mixture, by adding red or yellow, and thus give life or warmth to a picture. A painting or tint is said to be *cold,* when *blue* is the predominating color).

For the *second* shade of blue, mix prepared white, cobalt blue, and rose madder, using *more* white than for the darkest shade. For the *third,* and palest shade, seen near the horizon, and left-hand upper corner, mix prepared white, cobalt blue, and rose madder, using more white than with either the first or second shade. You should now compare these *three* shades with the distinct shades of blue, seen in the *cloudless sky*. Now begin applying the darkest shade of blue, using a flat bristle brush, and commencing at the top of the right hand corner; as you near the left hand side, add a little of the second shade of blue, blending each shade into the other by crossing the brush-strokes, thus : ✕ ✕ ✕ ✕.

Use the *second* shade for the middle part of the sky, adding a little of the *third* (lightest) shade where it begins to get lighter. As you near the left hand side and approach the horizon, use the lightest shade. Pass a clean, large, flat bristle brush over it lightly, in various directions, to remove the more prominent brush-marks. *Use plenty of paint*. When the sky is perfectly dry, "oil it out," by dipping a large, clean, flat bristle brush into poppy oil, and pass it quickly over the sky, rubbing the oil in well with the brush. A clean piece of old cotton is used to wipe it dry. The clouds are painted next. The proper shade for the brightest tints is obtained by mixing a very little vermilion with the prepared white. For the *darkest* shade, add a little light red and ivory black. The whitest portions of the clouds are represented by applying prepared white and blending it with the darker portions. Also blend parts of the clouds into the sky by dragging the edges together with a clean brush. Now paint the mountain. For the bluish portion, seen just above the tops of the trees, use the same colors that were used for the *darkest* shade of the sky, adding a very little light red. For the light part of the mountain, use the same tints as for the clouds.

We now come to a very important feature in landscape painting, namely, the foliage. It is very necessary that we represent the different varieties of trees as they appear to us in nature, so that we can readily tell to which class they belong. This is done by depicting their *general* appearance, shape, and *manner* of branching. But we must never attempt to paint foliage in such detail that the kind of tree is to be distinguished by the particular shape of its leaves, or color. Foliage should be laid in *first* in masses of light and shade, selecting a tone of each mass, which is *not* the *highest light* nor the darkest shadow, and then the details are painted by putting on the high lights, and the dark accents of shadow. ("High lights"—The lightest parts, caused by the light falling directly upon any object.) When you wish to give an appearance of light shining through or upon any part of foliage, paint such parts in a lighter shade and apply the paint thickly, giving it the rough, dotted appearance as shown in the colored study. This particular dotted effect is produced by using a small round brush, well filled with paint, and touching it lightly to the canvas and then raising it up again *without any attempt at making a stroke with the brush.* Let us begin with the foliage at the foot of the mountain. As these trees are away in the distance, and the greens have a sort of gray, cool appearance, we must strive to make them look distant in our painting, by painting them rather dimly, and with no attempt at detail.

To secure this effect, use for the dark shades terre verte, Naples yellow, a little ivory black and a little rose madder to warm

For the light tints use rose madder, yellow ochre and Naples yellow. Mix these colors loosely before putting them on, and use a round bristle-brush or worn sable for distant foliage. And for finishing touches use a small sable.

We now direct our attention to the evergreens in the middle distance. We find this group of trees a little more distinct; yet they are not sufficiently near us that any limbs can be seen. In fact, but a small portion of the trunks, in one or two of them, are even hinted at (*see study*). To paint this group, use ivory black, terre verte, raw sienna and a little light red to warm. Before painting the foliage in the foreground, we will paint the rough water that is shown so beautifully in the study before us. To do this nicely, you must exercise great care in getting the dark shades of water in their proper *form* and *place.* Lay in the dark shades first, using prepared white, bitumen, terre verte and a very little light red to warm. This done, take a dry, flat sable brush and dip it into prepared white, now spread out the hairs into a fan shape, by pulling them apart with your fingers, and drag this lightly over the water in the distance. But use *pure*

silver white, in the same manner, for the edges of foam. Before putting in the lights for the water, paint in the island and the land to the right and left. For the rocks use ivory black, silver white, and a little light red to warm. Use Vandyke brown for the darkest shades on the rocks.

In painting rocks, or any hard objects, we should endeavor to depict them so that they will look *decidedly hard*. Thus, again, in painting soft objects, such as fleecy clouds, foam, etc., we should give them the appearance of *unmistakable softness*. We will now begin painting the foliage in the foreground. For the darkest portions of foliage, use ivory black, yellow ochre, and a little burnt sienna. Where the lighter greens are seen in these evergreens, use light zinober green, mixing in a little of the dark green, which has just been used in painting the darker foliage, to avoid too great a contrast in the shades. For the lighter foliage of trees in the same groups, use Naples yellow, rose madder and a little vermilion, and *add a little of the light green which has been used for the light portion of the darkest foliage.* Mix them just enough to make them combine a little, and thus preserve their freshness. The finishing touches are applied after the first paintings are dry, by adding the high lights and dark accents of shadow, using the general tone of the masses as a foundation. The trunks of the trees may now be painted. Use bone brown for the darkest shades : and for the light shades use bone brown, adding a little white, and burnt sienna. Where the small branches are clearly indicated, draw them in with a fine-pointed brush, using bone brown. In other parts they are only hinted at, by using a lighter shade of paint.

In order to give the trunks of trees their natural *rounded appearance*, the *darkest part* of the shaded side should be removed a little from the edge : and so, also, with the *lightest* side of the *lightest part (where the light of the sun shines upon them)*, should be somewhat removed from the edge. Blend the lights and shades in the *middle* of the trunks. Notice this feature where it is shown in the trunks of trees seen in the foreground, at the right hand side of the colored study.

In painting water, whether in motion or stillness, do not make it too light for its surroundings, as this will throw the whole picture out of harmony.

Nothing adds to the beauty of a picture more than well painted water.   For the water *below* the falls use bitumen, terre verte, prepared white and a little light red.   Now take a flat brush and paint in the reflections or shadows of rocks and trees that show in the water, using the same colors as for the *objects reflected*. Do this with a *downward stroke of the brush*. The dim reflections of the clouds in the water are then laid on, using the same warm pink, but not so bright.   These are also painted in *downwards*, in the direction of the flowing water.   You then take a clean flat sable brush and *lightly* cross the downward strokes, used in painting the shadows and reflections, with horizontal strokes   This gives the shadows the appearance of being *under* the water.   Where the water breaks over the rocks, use *pure white* for the edges of spray ; but where the little white streaks are seen below the falls, use *prepared white*.

When the painting is dry, the details are then carried on ; finishing touches applied   re needed, the shadows strengthened, the lights touched up, etc. Lights   ed be painted very heavily and with a full brush of paint ; while the shadows should be thinner and transparent.   A careful examination of the colored study, where such parts on which the paints are applied thickly to the foliage and other parts, are indicated, will give a clear idea of the effect to be aimed at.

As all paints become more or less dull when thoroughly dry, something is needed to bring the colors back to their former brilliancy.   To accomplish this, we take one-third each of Siccative de Harlem, refined linseed oil and turpentine ; put this mixture on *thinly* with a brush, and wipe off any surplus drops with a clean rag.

Instructions for Painting
Vancouver View.

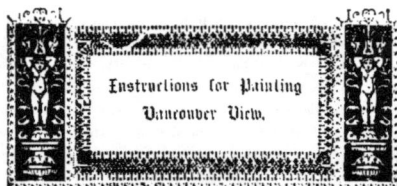

MANY of our best and most enterprising artists are beginning to make the magnificent mountain scenery of British Columbia and the Pacific Coast, a favorite sketching resort. The study under consideration is one of the many beautiful scenes that frequently meet the eye. Here, on every side, the mountains rise, in varied forms and in endless change of aspect, as the lights and shadows play upon their serrated peaks. The remarkable clearness of the air in this locality brings out the minutest detail of these dark blue specimens of nature's sculpture work. The study before us, "View of Vancouver," as seen from the residence of the governor of Vancouver Island, depicts a glorious group of opalescent peaks, fading into the distance against a ruddy sky. Those who cannot give these diversified scenes a personal visit, and feast their artistic tastes upon them, as they are seen in their natural beauty, will, we think, appreciate our efforts to bring a little of this mountain nature into our homes in the shape of a fac-simile of a real oil painting, designed and executed from nature.

We need hardly add, that the natural beauty of its position, its imposing appearance, and the majestic surroundings, all contribute towards making it a most interesting picture.

TRANSFERRING OR SKETCHING IN THE OUTLINES.

This may be successfully done by any of the methods described for the preceding study, "Les Chats Rapids." It is always better for the student to practise free-hand drawing, in making the first sketch for a painting, using a charcoal stick or crayon sharpened to a point. It will be surprising what accurate results will follow a little practice in this direction. If a mistake occurs, the charcoal can be readily rubbed off and the corrections made. *(See paragraph on " Comparative Measurement.")* Take some prominent object, or leading line in the study as your standard or starting point, and draw in all other objects, or lines in their proper relation to this starting point. In this case, it would be well to draw in the base line of the picture first, and then *the almost horizontal shore line* at the base of the mountain. This will form a foundation for the leading lines, which indicate the slopes of the lower portions of the mountain, as seen in the "Outline Sketch." These lines should be drawn in first commencing at the left hand side. Notice that they nearly all incline in one direction, namely, towards the left. When one or two lines are drawn, it will serve as a guide when drawing in others, which are placed in a certain relation to the last line drawn. Now mark off the lines which *slant* towards the right and those indicating the tops of the mountains. The smaller trees in the foreground may now be outlined. Notice that their tops terminate *quite near* the shore line at the ba   of the mountain. The very small trees are then sketched, in their proper relation, comparing *their heights* with that of the larger ones just drawn in. In this way one line or object is made to give a basis for others. A few lines to indicate the general form of the rocks in the foreground, the large tree, and the shapes of clouds, will complete the outlines. Now compare your charcoal sketch with the original, and if the proportions are all found to be correct, you should then follow the outlines with burnt sienna and turpentine. It is a good idea, when tracing

Outline Sketch of VANCOUVER VIEW.

the outlines, to use a *shade of paint* with the turpentine similar to the color of the object under consideration.

APPLYING THE PAINTS.

We see at a glance that the blue portion of the sky is very similar to that in "Les Chats Rapids," but having a trifle more ivory black mixed in for certain portions to give it the greyish appearance seen in this study. Prepare the *three* shades of blue in the same manner as for the preceding study, adding a little more ivory black in the darkest shade, in order to imitate the greyish-blue tint seen in certain parts. But apply and graduate the *lighter* shades of blue *towards the right hand side* in this study, instead of towards the left, as was done with "Les Chats Rapids." When this is dry, "oil it out," and then lay on the clouds in their proper form and place. Use, for the general tone, *prepared white (silver white mixed with a little yellow ochre)*, and a little vermilion. For the brightest tints, add a little rose madder. For the dark shades, add a very little light red and ivory black to the *darkest shade* of sky blue. If this be found too dark, add sufficient prepared white to make it light enough. Use a dry brush to blend the lights and shades together. Also blend in a little rose pink just above the mountains.

Next in order, comes the peaks of the distant mountains. To paint the *darkest sides* of these peaks, we will take from the plat of paint the darkest mixture of blue used in painting the sky, and to this we will add a little red to warm. This will give you a tint that will give the dark sides of peaks *a rather bluer* appearance than is seen in the study, and it is to be preferred. For the *light sides* of peaks, use a pale pink and white, making those peaks near the large tree more grey in quality by the addition of a little ivory black. For the darker portions of the mountain, nearer the water, use bone brown, cobalt blue and a little light red; and mix in *prepared white* to lighten the shades. For the light tints, use prepared white, light red and a little rose madder.

In painting the water, use the same tints as for the mountain, painting the *shadows downward*. Then lightly cross these shadows *horizontally*.

using the light pink cloud tints to reflect the clouds. A little of the *lightest shade* of the sky blue is applied in the same manner to reflect the small blue portions seen in the water near the foregrounds. Lay on the little white streaks with the palest pink shade. The application of these reflections in light *horizontal brush strokes*, painted upon the *downward strokes*, (in which the shadows of the mountains have first been painted in) has the *desired effect of representing the shadows of the mountains as being under water.* (The method of producing this particular effect, though simple, is known to few). We will now suppose the sky, clouds, mountains and water to be dry, after which we will paint the evergreens in the foreground, using on the darkest shades of foliage, ivory black, cadmium and a little light red. For the light foliage add a little light zinober green *to the green just used for the darker portion.* Use, for the bright tints, Naples yellow, yellow ochre and rose madder. For the rich brown shades, use burnt umber and a little burnt sienna. For the small black markings that indicate the trunks of the trees, use Vandyke brown. We will now direct our attention to the strip of ground lying between the small trees and the layers of rocks in the immediate foreground. To imitate this grassy appearance faithfully will afford us another new lesson on "the knack of handling the brush," which we will explain before going further. The color for grass is laid in by using a small round bristle brush and *touching it lightly to the canvas, or mill board, and quickly jerking the brush upward,* which will produce a free, natural appearance of irregular grass. You must always commence at the most distant portion and *work towards* you, using more paint, and thus give more prominence to the grass as you near the foreground. In this case, mix, for the first painting of the ground, raw umber, a little Vandyke brown, and a very little burnt sienna; lighten this mixture by mixing in prepared white and Naples yellow. Mix them with a palette knife, and only enough to make them combine a little, and apply this paint in the manner described, thus giving it a grassy appearance from the start. Be sure you *commence* this painting at the foot of the trees near the water, *and work towards the foreground,* as it is impossible to properly

ドイツ中部ハルツ地方の針葉樹林

perform the jerking of the brush upwards if you were to attempt to begin
at the foreground and work backwards, towards the distance. When this
is dry put in finishing touches where needed, painting in the grass in the
foreground more prominently, imitating the yellowish green and brownish
effects s 1 in the study. The distant trees, to the right, are the next
objects painted, for which use, for the lightest shade, a little rose madder
with a pale green tint, *made by adding a little prepared white to the green
already used for the foliage in the foreground.* Add raw umber where a
darker shade is required. Begin the large oak tree by drawing in (with
a small round bristle brush) the trunk and branches, using raw umber and
ivory black, adding yellow ochre for the brighter touches. The proportions
of these colors must of course be varied to match the different portions
under consideration, using less of one color and more of another as necessity
suggests. As the dark greens in this tree are almost identical with the
dark shade seen in the larger evergreens to the right, we, therefore, prepare
a similar shade for this one, using ivory black, light cadmium, and a little
light red. Using burnt sienna and a very little vermilion to give it the
rich brown appearance. A few touches of Vandyke brown, applied here
and there, will darken the shady side. Use Naples yellow and pink for
the light tints on the foliage, branches and trunk.

The rocks in the foreground are painted in last. Use for the general
tone ivory black, prepared white and a little light red. For the dark
shades use Vandyke brown. For the lightest tints mix Naples yellow, silver
white and a very little vermilion. Lay on the lights thickly. When the
rocks are dry, drag a little bright green over parts of the rocks, to imitate
the moss shown in the study. With a little darker shade of green paint
in the little bushes that are seen at the edges of the rock. Now look
carefully over your painting and compare it with the study before you, and
add finishing touches where needed.

The practice from these studies, and according to the instructions of this
and preceding chapters, will enable the reader to readily express nearly all the
varied effects of nature. When the reader has gained the knowledge of colors

and attained the proficiency of "handling the brush" that the study of these instructions will give, he should begin at once to paint landscapes from nature.

MOUNTING THE COLORED STUDIES.

The colored studies of this book are such perfect representations of real oil paintings, that many of our patrons may wish to mount them, or others, upon canvas, or muslin, instead of painting them; to such the following hints will prove valuable: Make a stretcher, according to directions given on page 24, and tack upon this stretcher cheap unbleached muslin or linen, stretching it tightly.   Now varnish it all over on the back with coach varnish, and let it dry for a couple of days.   Then make a paste of silver gloss starch, putting into a teacupful of starch about a teaspoonful of white gum arabic, dissolved in water.   Stir it until cold; spread it on the canvas very thinly and also on the back of the picture.   Place the picture on the canvas and rub with a cloth until it sticks; then hang it up to dry.   Great care must be taken to keep the canvas and edges rubbed down smoothly.   The sizing or paste must be put on quickly, or it will set before the picture is put on.   The advantage of this sizing is that it will draw as tight as a drum, and will not stain the most delicate pictures.

HOW TO MAKE VARNISH FOR THE COLORED MOUNTED STUDIES.

This varnish is the same as that used for all fine chromos.   It will not lose its lustre by steam, or by rubbing with a cloth wet with cold water to clean it, and is made as follows: Take best coach varnish one part and alcohol two parts; put them in a bottle, and shake them.   Then pour a little into a cup, take a camel's hair brush, such as is used for varnishing, and spread on quickly, for the alcohol will evaporate very soon.   The varnish must be shaken every time it is poured out, as the alcohol will not stay mixed with the varnish.   If one coat will not do, put on another in a day or two after the first has dried, brushing it the other way on the picture.   This gives a beautiful polish, if care is taken to keep it out of the dust while drying. Another method of varnishing a mounted chromo is as follows: Take a clean flat varnish brush and lay on an even coat of size, made by dissolving white glue or isinglass in luke-warm water till it becomes of the consistency of cold starch, going over the picture lightly and evenly. When quite dry, go over it again in the same manner with Demar varnish, giving one or more coats, in a warm room. Lay it away out of the dust for a day or two, and your picture is ready to be hung up.

HOW TO HANG PICTURES.

To many, it may seem a very simple matter to hang pictures, but how few rooms there are in which they are hung so as to show their beauty. At fine art exhibitions they are frequently hung as though to fill up space. In hanging pictures, much depends upon individual taste; some will have the bottom of the picture frames on a line around the room, while others prefer to see it broken. Never hang a picture so that the shadows will come near a window, as the side that needs the light will not get it, and thus a good subject may be spoiled, and the owner not know why. Do not hang small pictures above large ones, for small objects have to be nearer the eye to be seen well, while large subjects look better a short distance away. Pictures should never be hung opposite windows if it can be avoided, as both glass and varnish reflect the light, so that when standing in front of them it almost totally hides the picture.

Always be sure that the cord and nails are strong enough to sustain their weight. Select a cord as near the color of the walls as possible. When pictures are hung in more than one row, have the top ones lean forward more than the lower ones; this can be done by putting the screw-eyes nearer the bottom in the sides of the frame. When common cord is used it should be examined once every few months, as the weight of the picture cuts the cord where it crosses the nail, and by not taking this precaution, many pictures have been ruined by falling. Wire cord is best, but it must be watched also. Never hang paintings and chromos side by side, but put engravings between. Do not hang water-colors near oil paintings, chromos, or other colored pictures. Have the best pictures you can afford, as one good picture is worth a dozen poor ones. Landscapes make a room look larger than other pictures; full length, or large sized animals should not be hung with smaller subjects, as giants and pigmies give too much contrast, and are not pleasant to the sight.

ADDITIONAL HINTS CONCERNING OIL PAINTINGS AND ENGRAVINGS.

Heavy gilt frames only are appropriate for oil paintings. Gilt frames, if varnished when new, can be washed without injury. Oil paintings can be washed in sweet milk and warm water, then carefully dried; do not rub them hard.

Castile soap and water can be used on oil paintings without danger, care being taken, of course, not to wet the back, or let the water through cracks. For ordinary dusting of pictures, a silk handkerchief should be used.

When discolored by age, they have been restored, by brushing them free from dust and then covering by a layer of shaving soap for a few minutes, after which they are thoroughly dried and soaked in nitro-glycerine.

Water, in which onions have been soaked, rubbed lightly over the frames, will keep flies from them.

An engraving would be made to appear cold by a bright or heavy gilt frame, though sometimes a plain unburnished one looks well. Of course a margin of white paper is needed between the printed surface and the frame, so as not to make the contrast of the brilliancy too violent.

Moleskin Velvet, or Shadow Painting.

By MINNIE CROX WHEELER.

THE instructions for this new method of painting on moleskin velvet appears in print for the first time, and no doubt many will be eager to learn it. It is decidedly a new idea in painting, having been recently introduced into the Kensington Art School. The work is very smooth and leaves as fine a surface upon the velvet as water colors do upon paper, thus differing from any other method of velvet painting. The paints used are the oil paints, same as used for landscape painting, but mixed with turpentine. The colors are put on thinly, and with *round* sable brushes, afterwards trimmed as shown in the illustration. With these the colors are *rubbed* into the velvet rather than painted on the surface, as the color diluted with turpentine acts like a dye, and, if properly done, the pile of the velvet will not be crushed at all, and when finished no brush marks will be seen.

Another peculiarity about this painting is that no palette is used to hold the paints, but they are placed on the *edges* of small butter plates, the bottom and side of the plates being used to hold the turpentine and to mix the paints. The moleskin velvet comes in three shades, namely: white, cream and coffee-color, costing about $1.75 per yard in the best quality, and when painted upon, can be used for the greatest variety of decorative purposes — banners, panels, bracket drapes, strips in sofa cushions, and for covering wooden plaques, etc.   The instructions are written for the white velvet, but, by being slightly modified, they are applicable to any of the three units.

MATERIALS.

The materials required for the two colored studies are: *Round* sable brushes, paints, refined turpentine, a few small butter plates, a piece of soft cotton and powdered charcoal for stamping.   Do *not* attempt to use stamping powder for this work, as it will not whisk off the velvet after the outlines are traced with paint and turpentine.   It is important that no black powder should show through the paints

The paints required are black lead, flake white, geranium lake, carmine, cobalt, violet carmine, mauve (Nos. 1 and 2), and chrome yellow (No. 1). The brushes to be used are:

2 Round Sable Brushes, No. 5		2 Round Sable Brushes, No. 6	
4 " " No. 8		1 Camel's Hair	No. 4
1 " " No. 10		2 " "	No. 1

MAKING THE PATTERNS AND STAMPING THE OUTLINES.

Our first work will be to get the outlines of the study upon our velvet. This may be done by free hand drawing, using a stick of charcoal sharpened to a point.   But the quickest and most accurate way, for beginners, is to make a perforated pattern of the outline sketch that accompanies the colored studies. To do this, remove the outline sketch from the book and place it upon two or three folds of felt or flannel, and carefully prick out the outlines with a fine needle, care being taken that the perforations are made quite close, and the needle held perpendicular while making them.   Then place the pattern in position on the velvet (*smooth side up*), and hold both firmly on the table by placing a pin in each corner.   When this has been done, sprinkle a little of the powdered charcoal over the pattern, and rub gently with a small piece of felt or flannel.   If care has been taken in perforating, and the pattern removed carefully, you will have a perfect outline.

TRACING THE OUTLINES WITH PAINT.

You now take a fine camel's hair brush and trace out the charcoal outlines of leaves and flowers in their respective colors, using paint mixed with turpentine. For the leaves and stems, use a green tint mixed with turpentine; for the pansies, use light mauve mixed with turpentine. Outline the roses with geranium lake and turpentine. For the forget-me-nots, make a pale shade of blue by mixing white and cobalt blue with turpentine. Make the paint outlines of the lightest tint seen in the study, and not too distinct or heavy. Be careful that those outlines which indicate where the lights meet the shadows, and those that denote the turning of leaf or petal, are placed in their proper form and position. Strive to have an accurate outline throughout, and then you will be able to devote full attention to coloring. When the paint outlines are finished, you then brush off the charcoal outlines with a broom whisk. The charcoal outlines will all dust off *from beneath* the paint outlines, not leaving the slightest trace of charcoal. This is a very important item. But if ordinary stamping powder were used instead of charcoal, it *would not* dust off after the paint outlines were traced upon it; hence the necessity of using powdered charcoal (which can be had from any druggist)

Now place the traced velvet on light brown paper, turning the paper over close to the tracing and tack with a fine white thread, in order that the velvet may be kept clean as well as firm.

HOW TO TRIM THE BRUSHES.

The brushes, with the exception of one No. 6 sable, which is used as a striper, are trimmed with a sharp pair of scissors, in the following manner: begin by cutting a few hairs quite close to the handle, all around the brush; now clip off another round of hairs a little nearer the point of the brush; continue the clipping process on the same principle as you would sharpen a pencil, until the hairs are nicely rounded and terminating *almost* to a point, as shown in the illustration. As the handles of brushes are much too long for use in velvet painting, it would be advisable to break off a portion.

The paints are seldom mixed together, and there must be a brush for every different color, as it is impossible to keep the short brushes clean, and too much washing wears them out ; the secret of your success being nice clean brushes and dishes, and the proper use of turpentine.

In order that all may clearly understand the terms used in the following instructions, we give

THE NAMES OF THE DIFFERENT PARTS OF A FLOWER.

Calyx—The cup surrounding the corolla. The parts of a calyx are called sepals.

Corolla—The blossom, the parts of which are called petals.

Stamens—Are found within the corolla ; they are a number of thread-like organs, the parts of which are the anther, pollen, and filament.

Pistil—The central organ of the flower ; its parts are the ovary, style and stigma.

Receptacle—The receptacle is the end of the stem which supports the other parts or organs of the flower.

The parts of the Calla Lily are the *spatha* and *spadix*. The former is the blossom , the latter is the central organ.

LAYING IN THE SHADOWS.

Where there are very light flowers, such as calla lilies, Easter lilies, etc., it is necessary to paint a little shadow around them and outside their outlines. To make this shading, put a little black lead on the edge of your saucer and a small quantity of turpentine into the saucer ; then take a camel's hair brush, No. 4, and merely touch the black lead with it and stir it into the turpentine, having another saucer at hand containing clean turpentine ; now brush around the flowers, forming a nice grey shadow, being careful *not to let the shadow run into the flowers and surrounding leaves ;* then dip your brush into the clean

turpentine and blend the edges out softly to the white velvet, as shown in
Easter lilies in the second study.

HOW TO COLOR THE FLOWERS.

For the "Calla Lily" put a little cobalt on the edge of your saucer,
also a small quantity of black lead, and with your No. 8 brush merely
touch the blue and then the black lead and mix in turpentine ; after shading
the flower, blend out with clean turpentine in the same way as for the
shading described in the preceding paragraph. This being done, take another
brush, No. 8, and paint the pistil with chrome yellow and shade with burnt
sienna.   To make the white rolled edge you may always use the brush
that has been used in applying the black lead by washing the black well out.
Put some flake white on the edge of a clean saucer and mix with a couple
of drops of clean turpentine, now wipe the brush clean and take up a
little white paint on the side of the brush; turn the brush so that the paint
is touching the edge of flower, then roll or turn the brush slowly, holding the
handle easy between the thumb and forefinger, always keeping the brush
inside the flower.   As it is difficult to manipulate the brush in the sharp
angles, the pen may then be used instead, holding it in your hand the
same as for writing ; place the point of the pen on the line of the design
with the edge side of the pen under (instead of the hollow side under
as in writing), and the hollow side of pen facing outside of the pattern.   Then,
as you draw the pen toward you in making the roll, gradually turn it so
that the hollow side would come under (as in writing)

For the rose, take geranium lake, mixed in a small quantity of
turpentine, and with a camel's hair brush, No. 1, lay in a rich crimson
tint.   Now take a sable brush, No. 8, and shade with carmine ; then with
brush, No. 5. paint a light touch of violet carmine in the darker places, in
order to get a deeper color.   For the bud, use the same brushes and
colors, omitting the violet carmine.   To make the moss on the bud, take
a No. 10 brush and use green No. 1, shading with burnt sienna and green
No. 2.   Now take the striper dip it into burnt sienna and turpentine

mixed, but not too thinly, and paint in the fine brown markings of the bud, using a little green No. 2 occasionally, as seen in the study.

For the pansies use brush No. 8. The yellow centres of all of them are painted first, using lemon yellow and turpentine. For the dark pansy, at the left-hand side, use violet, carmine and black lead in the darker places. On the turned edges a little white is afterwards applied. Paint the dark portions of the yellow centres with burnt sienna, and use violet carmine for the fine markings that radiate from the centres of the pansies, using the striper, and always commencing from the centre, and making the markings downwards in quick strokes. Put in the white spots, seen in the centre of the pansies, with a pen, using white paint. Just below these white spots, a very small speck of red and green, mixed, is also put on with a pen. For the light pansy use mauve No. 1, and with brush No. 10 touch very lightly to the color and mix in turpentine Shade with the same color, using brush No. 5. The lower pansy is painted with mauve No. 2, the same as the light one, but in this case use more color and less turpentine. Paint the buds with the same color.

For the calla lily leaf use brush No. 10, with chrome green No. 1, and a little burnt sienna and chrome yellow near the top. Shade with green No. 2 and burnt sienna, using brush No. 6 in forming veins The leaves are painted with chrome yellow, carmine, burnt sienna, and green No. 1, being careful not to mix, but let the colors blend into each other; shade and form veins with brush No. 6; then dip the striper into the violet carmine, and paint fine veins over those just made. Paint the stems with the striper, also the fern, using the same color as that used for leaves.

For the forget-me-nots use flake white and cobalt, mixed with a little turpentine. Cut the hair *squarely* off an old sable brush, close to the handle, dip in color, and place on the velvet directly on the spot where the flower is wanted; bear with considerable pressure on the brush, and at the same time give it a slight twist. Put in the yellow centres with the pen. The little pink spots are put in with light touches of geranium lake. The buds of the forget-me-not are painted with geranium lake and white mixed.

INSTRUCTIONS FOR THE STUDY OF TEA ROSES, EASTER LILIES AND FUCHSIAS.

The *shading around the outside* of the outlines of flowers is applied first, and in the same manner as described for the preceding study; so, also, the shading and roll edge on the Easter lily is done in the same way as described for the calla lily. After the background shadows are laid on in their proper place, begin by painting the centre of the Easter lily, using a tinge of No. 1 green, and blend it out lightly near the edge, as seen in the study. Now paint the stamens with geranium lake, using the striper. The tops of the stamens are painted with burnt sienna. The long pistil is painted green. Paint the pink rose with geranium lake, using a No. 1 camel's hair brush; touch the brush very lightly in the color and mix in turpentine to a delicate tint, being careful not to have the brush *too full* when applying the paint, as there is danger of it spreading. Shade the rose *(or blend it out with the white velvet)* with the same color, but apply very sparingly in the light portions. Use brush No. 8 for this shading process. The buds are painted in the same color, and finished up with moss in the same way as the preceding study. In painting the yellowish tea rose, use the brush that has been used in applying the white paint; with this brush the background shadows are laid in, using cobalt and black lead in the same way as directed for the calla lily in the preceding study. This done, put some English vermilion and lemon yellow on the edge of the plate, mix in a very little of the vermilion with the yellow and turpentine and paint it all over, just letting the color blend into the dark background shading. Where the brighter tints are seen, vermilion alone is used. For the fuchsias, use mauve No. 1, and brushes Nos. 10 and 5. Paint with the large brush and shade with the smaller one. Then roll on the edge in the same way as for the lilies, using the pen for the points; then in the brush used for green paints, and with No. 1 green, shade the white portion of the fuchsias into a delicate tinge of green, and paint that part next the green (as seen in the study). Paint the stamens with geranium lake, using the striper. The leaves, stems and forget-me-nots are painted in the same way as described for the preceding study.

INSTRUCTIONS FOR PAINTING THE ROSE AND BLUEBELL STUDY.

The tracing of the design, perforating the pattern, stamping it, and painting the outlines, is done in the same manner as given in the instructions for the colored studies. But if the reader does not wish to use the outline designs, or the sketches that accompany the colored studies, as patterns from which to stamp, she may resort to the following plan, which is just as good as using the original, and very little extra work : Take a *thin* piece of paper, and with a piece of cloth rub it all over with powdered charcoal ; shake off all surplus powder. You then place this powdered sheet upon a piece of fine writing paper (powdered side facing the writing paper). Now place these *two* sheets under the outline design in the book, and with a knitting-needle, or tracing point, carefully follow the outlines of the engraving ; this causes the powder to come off the powdered sheet upon the writing paper in outline. You have now simply to trace out the powdered outlines with a pencil, and perforate *this*, instead of the outline sketches that are bound in the book. (For additional hints on *transferring, tracing*, etc., see page 41).

The same paints and brushes that were used with the preceding studies are used, with the addition of sable brushes Nos. 10, 6 and 5, and a tube of magenta and carmine. The centre rose may be a dark one, and painted according to the directions given for the dark rose in the first study. The one at the side is a *tea rose*, and the lower one a *light pink*. (See instructions on the *second* study for directions how to paint a tea rose and a pink rose). I painting the bluebells, use brush No. 6, and mix a little cobalt in a small quantity of turpentine, using a little more color for shading in the darker places. The lower pansy may be painted with violet carmine, and the upper one with magenta No. 1, according to the directions given for colored study.

INSTRUCTIONS FOR PANSY STUDY.

In all pansies the yellow centres are painted first. Those pansies which are shown dark in the engraving may be painted violet carmine, sometimes painting a little vermilion under the edge of the violet carmine that be cover the yellow portion. (See *colored study of Roses and Pansies*)

ROSE DESIGN

A pansy painted in burnt sienna and shaded with carmine, is pretty for a variety. For a magenta colored pansy, use brush No. 10, first, and apply the magenta rather thinly over the yellow centres; in the other portions of it use plenty of paint, giving the pansy a rich color, then shade with the same color, using brush No. 5; put in the *little* spots in the centre of the pansy with a pen, using burnt sienna. Take violet carmine, and, with a striper, put in all the fine markings that radiate from the centres of the pansies. For a light yellow pansy, use the brush that has been used in applying white paint. Shade in the dark places with black lead and cobalt mixed with turpentine, and paint the remainder with lemon yellow. The small spots are put in with burnt sienna, and the striping with violet carmine.

For a dark yellow pansy, use a little cadmium mixed in turpentine and shade with same color, using a little burnt sienna in the darker places, the spots are put on with burnt sienna and striping with violet carmine.

For the backs of the pansies, paint a little yellow close around the green portion where the stems terminate, and the remainder with mauve No. 1 or 2, shading with a little of same color; the balance of pansies and buds may be painted with mauve No. 1 or 2, shading with a little more of same color.

The leaves should be shaded a trifle darker than those in the colored designs. If the upper flowers be painted in the light colors and the lower ones dark, the subject will have a better appearance.

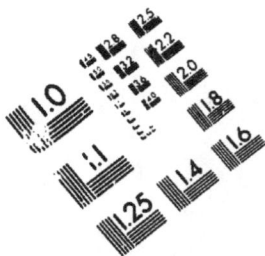

IMAGE EVALUATION
TEST TARGET (MT-3)

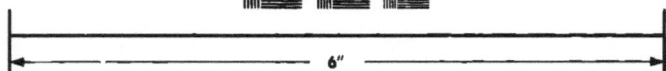

6"

Photographic
Sciences
Corporation

23 WEST MAIN STREET
WEBSTER, N.Y. 14580
(716) 872 4503

Progressive Art Needle-Work.

THE Progressive method of teaching Art Needle-work will be found far in advance of any means employed in other publications. We are proud to say that it is a commendable departure from the antiquated, wearisome methods formerly employed. Instructions on this useful and fascinating branch of art-work, shown in different degrees of completion, cannot but possess advantages peculiarly its own, and be welcomed by all. The writer seems to have been aware of the many discouraging failures of those who tried to make satisfactory progress by the old methods in other books, with *small* designs, and has hit upon a *new plan*, which will overcome all difficulties and possess every advantage of personal lessons. The plan is to give, in a concise form, *the latest* designs in full sized working patterns, and plainly show, in the same illustration, *all* the stitches that are used in working each design, and thus enable the reader to see at a glance how to utilize the stitches in their proper place. Whereas, with other methods of book instruction, the stitches were jumbled together, good, bad and indifferent, and the reader was left at a loss to know how, or where, to utilize them. But the plan adopted in this chapter fully overcomes these defects, by illustrating, in each design, all the stitches that are used in working it ; and the needle is inserted in the proper place and the *correct* slant indicated, so that the reader can readily see just where to take the next stitch. Another defect of other books is, that the designs

were so small, that they were utterly useless; in this, however, we have all
the designs and patterns in *full size*, ready to be perforated and stamped upon
the material without the tedious task of enlarging. The first work to be done
is to learn

HOW TO MAKE PERFORATED PATTERNS AND DO THE STAMPING.

To do this, procure a piece of American bond paper (or thin writing
paper), 12 x 14 inches, and make it transparent by rubbing it all over thinly
with clarified linseed oil. Hang it up to dry; it takes some time to dry, but
must be thoroughly dried before using. Paper thus prepared is called Tracing
Paper. You have now merely to place this paper over the engraved design,
and with a lead pencil trace out the outlines with a steady hand. The design
being accurately traced, the pattern is ready to be perforated. Lay a couple
of folds of cloth on the table, place the traced pencil sketch upon this, and
with a needle of medium size prick out the pattern, being careful to follow the
outlines and make the perforations quite close. By placing three or four sheets
of paper under the traced sketch and pinning them together, a number of patterns can be pricked at once. Place the perforated pattern (rough side up)
on the material to be stamped, placing heavy weights on the corner to keep
it from slipping; then rub stamping powder over the perforations with a piece
of felt till the pattern is clearly marked on the material (this can be ascer-
tained by lifting one corner of the pattern slightly). Then remove the pattern
carefully. Lay a piece of thin paper over the stamping and pass a hot iron
over it; this melts the gum in the powder and fastens the pattern to the material. The iron should be as hot as possible without scorching the cloth.
Should the heat change the color of the material, iron it all over. Do not do
any stamping by this process on a hot or damp day if it can be avoided.
Keep the powder in a cool, dry place. In stamping with light colored powders, the best way to fasten it is to hold the back of the cloth against a stove
pipe or the face of the iron. French stamping is better, however, for all dark
materials. To take the powder up on the distributor, have a tin plate with a
piece of woollen cloth glued on the bottom, sprinkle a little powder on the

cloth and rub the distributor over it, taking care to shake off all the powder you can ; enough will remain to stamp the pattern clearly.

To Make a Distributor.—Take a strip of fine felt, about an inch wide (a strip from an old felt hat is as good as anything), roll it up tightly into a roll, leaving the end flat, and rub the end over a piece of sand-paper, to make it sm.ooth and even.

To Make Blue Powder.—Take equal parts of pulverized gum damar and white rosin, and just enough Persian blue to color it ; mix well together.

Other Colors are made in the same way, using for coloring chrome yellow (for light colored powder), burnt sienna, lamp black, etc. Black powder is improved by adding a little blue to it.

To Make White Powder.—Take one ounce of white lead, half an ounce of gum arabic in the impalpable powder, half an ounce of white rosin in the fine powder ; mix well together.

Superior Dark Blue Powder.—One ounce white rosin, one-half ounce gum sandarac, one-half ounce Prussian blue in fine powder; **mix all thoroughly**.

Black Liquid Stamping is made by putting a very little lamp black into a bottle containing benzine. Put in just enough to make it a pale black when shaken. This makes an excellent stamping liquid, as it dries as soon as applied, and will not rub off ; and the patterns need no cleaning after they are used ; it must be kept corked to prevent evaporation, and *away from the fire.* It is used in the following manner : Take an empty spool (plug up the hole with wood) and make a distributor, by folding two or three ply of felt over one end, leaving the felt long enough to overlap part of the side of the spool, securing the felt .o the spool by winding it with twine. You now place the felt end of the spool to the mouth of the bottle, and tip it upward a number of times till the distributor is well saturated. Now place the perforated pattern upon the material to be stamped (smooth side up) and rub the saturated distributor over the perforations.

French Indelible Stamping.—This is the best process for all dark materials. By this process a kind of paint is used instead of powder, and a square-end brush instead of a distributor. Place the pattern on the cloth, smooth side up if you can, though either side will work well, weight the pattern down as in stamping. Rub the paint evenly over the perforations, and it will leave the lines distinct. The paint is mixed in the following manner: Take zinc white, mix it with boiled oil to about the thickness of cream, add a little drying, such as painters use. Keep in a tin pail (one holding about a pint is a good size), have a piece of board cut round, with a screw in the centre for a handle, to fit *loosely* into the pail; drop this on the paint and it will keep it from drying up; add a little oil occasionally to keep the paint from getting too thick, and it will always be ready for use. After the stamping is done, the pattern must be *cleaned immediately;* this is done by placing the pattern on the table and turning benzine or naphtha over it to cut the paint, and then wiping the pattern *dry on both sides* with an old cloth. Do not use the pattern for powder stamping immediately after it has been used for the paint.

INSTRUCTIONS FOR MAKING SCOTCH THISTLE DESIGN.

This new method of working the thistle has the advantages of representing it faithfully, and of being very easily and rapidly done. It looks exceedingly pretty worked or painted on white velvet, or light colored felt; made up into a wall banner, having plush sewed to the ends, and finished with pon-pons. Be careful to select a shade of plush and pon-pons that will harmonize with the material upon which you work. A brass rod and rings will complete the mountings. This design enlarged, would look pretty for sofa cushions, etc. Make a pattern from the engraving, and stamp the design upon the velvet or felt, in the manner already described. This done, sew the material into an embroidery frame, and begin by working the stems with olive green embroidery silk with the *stem stitch*, giving the stitches the *upward slant* as shown in the illustration. Our engraving represents the work in different degrees of completion, and illustrates all the stitches used in working. Now fill in the lower part (or bulb) of each blossom with a grey shade of Berlin wool, as shown in the engraving of the large blossom. Double the yarn and repeat the stitches till you give the bulb a natural, rounded appearance. This done, fill in three rows of French knots (just

above the bulb, as seen in the large blossom), using the same shade of
yarn as for the bulb. This furnishes a foundation for the mauve filloselle,
which is next sewed down between the knots, in the following manner a
needle is threaded with strong thread; bring the needle up between the
upper row of knots. Now place a double strand of mauve (a thistle pink)
filloselle on the knots close to the thread; pass the needle back through
the material, catching the filloselle about three-quarters of an inch from one
end, draw the needle tightly. This has a tendency to make the filloselle
stand out straight, and as you do *not* want this effect for the thistle, you
at once see that something more is needed to make the filloselle lay *flat*
to the velvet; hence we take another fastening stitch (as shown in the
illustration) and catch both strands of the filloselle a *little* above the last
stitch. The long end of the filloselle, seen in the engraving, is then clipped
with a sharp pair of scissors, and this operation is repeated till three rows
of filloselle are sewed down. A glance at the finished blossom in the engraving will give an idea of the effect aimed at. The leaves are worked with
a greyish green arrasene. Begin working at the bottom of the leaf, and
slant the stitches upward, as shown in the leaf partly worked. The arrasene
stitch is so plainly illustrated, that it will be readily learned by any one.
A large wool needle is threaded with arrasene and brought up through the
material at the centre of the leaf; pass the needle down at the edge of
the leaf (see illustration), then bring it up again at the edge of the leaf;
now take the needle down at the centre of the leaf, and so on. By working in this manner, no arrasene is wasted on the under side. Work one-
half of the leaf first and then the other, working from the centre to the
outside in both cases. The lines seen in two of the leaves show the slant
and about the distance one stitch should be from the other. The leaves being
worked and the upper parts of the blossoms being filled in with filloselle, now
begin to cover the yarn foundation of each bulb (as seen in the large blossom)
with the same shade of arrasene as for the leaves, taking the stitches in the
same direction as those of the yarn foundation. Work the arrasene quite
closely, so that none of the yarn foundation will show through. Bring the

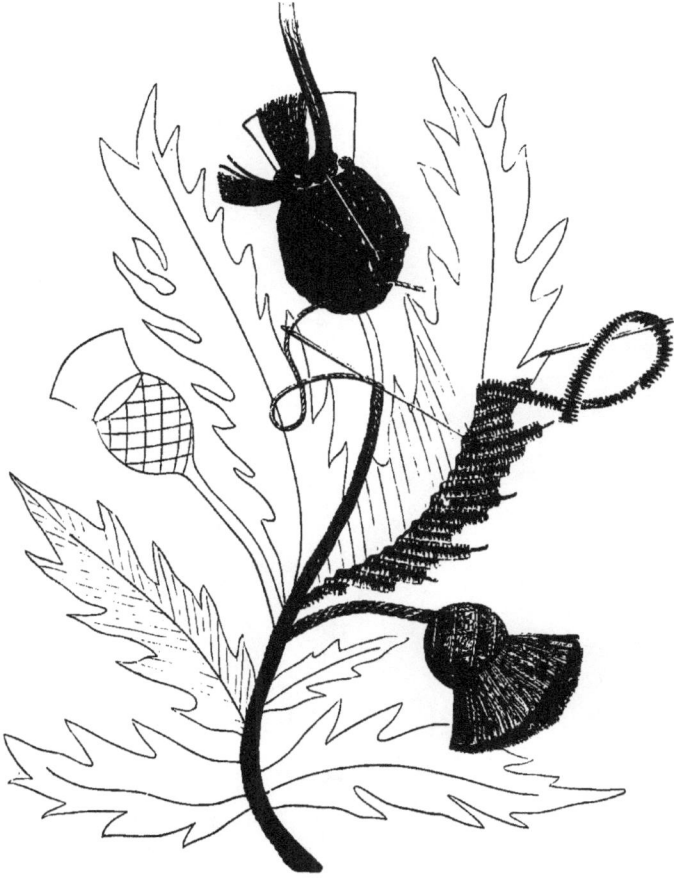

arrasene up so as to catch the lower part of the filloselle which forms the blossom. Now thread a fine needle with olive green etching silk and carry long stitches back and forth, diagonally across the top of the arrasene bulb, as seen in the finished blossom; and with the same shade make short stitches here and there to represent the thorns on the leaf, as seen in the partly finished leaf. Now comb out the blossoms to give them a downy appearance, and trim off the ends of the blossom, and your work is ready to be made up into any article that fancy might suggest.

INSTRUCTIONS FOR DOGWOOD BLOSSOM DESIGN.

This graceful design of Dogwood blossoms is well adapted to the greatest variety of decorative purposes: bracket-drapes, wall banners, sofa cushions, and plush mirror frames. It is very effective if worked on garnet or dark blue plush or felt. While any colored felt or plush is in taste, yet it will be readily understood by those who have studied decorative effect, why a dark tone is preferred—one does not weary of it, as would be the case with a light tint.

The flowers are a creamy white, with yellowish-brown centres, and little reddish-brown markings in the notches on the outside edge of the petals. The leaves are a medium shade of rather a warm, yellowish green. These features we must, of course, try and imitate in our needle-work.

The perforated pattern is made from the accompanying design, in the manner already described. If it be worked on plush, the French indelible stamping should be used, instead of the powdered process. We will now suppose that the design is stamped and the material placed in a good sized embroidery frame, when you will begin working the stems in olive green embroidery floss, in the same manner described and illustrated for the Poppy design, giving it the upward slant.

It may be of service to some of our readers, who may not have ready access to stores where embroidery frames are sold, to know how to make this useful article. A very serviceable frame can be readily made from two pieces of barrel-hoop, about three feet in length, cut down to one-half its usual width and thickness. The ends of the hoops are so beveled, that where the two ends overlap each other, they will be about the same thickness as the rest. It will be necessary to put the dry hoop into a pan of hot water, so that it will bend readily into place. The edges are then slightly notched in two places near the ends, and the hoop is bent round and the ends secured by wrapping twine in the notches. One hoop is, of course, made shorter and smaller than the other, so that it will fit neatly inside the other. The material to be embroidered is now placed over the smaller hoop, and the larger one is forced over the cloth and the smaller hoop, thus firmly securing the material to be embroidered. As they cost but 15 cents, few will take the trouble of making them, if procurable at the stores.

The leaves are worked in three shades of green arrasene. Select shades that partake of a yellowish-green cast, and as you near the top of the spray, use more of the lighter shades. The method of working and shading with arrasene is clearly illustrated and explained in the Fuchsia design, and the directions that follow. The sepals, that show on the back of some of the blossoms and buds, are also worked in green arrasene. The veins are put in after the leaves are finished, using rker shade of embroidery floss, or veining chenille. The petals may l   ced in two shades of cream white arrasene, or in two shades of white ribbosene, using the darker shade near the centre. (Ribbosene is a new material for embroidery. It is a cross between arrasene and ribbon, and yet unlike either. It is in fact similar to narrow ribbon, but is all silk and more elastic being crimped or waved. It is used only in making flowers).

Begin at the outside of the flowers, and work the stitches in the same way as shown in the illustrated Poppy design. The anthers, near the centre of the flowers, are made with a number of French knots in dark yellow embroidery floss, having some knots made with seal brown floss. The knot stitch is made in the following manner : Thread a common needle with yellow floss, and bring it up through the material, *from the under side*, at the point where the knot is wanted. Now catch the floss with your left hand, about *two inches* from the material upon which you embroider ; then hold the needle in your right hand, quite close to the material, and *with the left hand* wind

the floss twice around the point of the needle. Now insert the needle at about the same place it came up. Draw the floss down towards the point of the needle, and hold it tightly with the left hand as you take the needle back through the material at about the same point it came up. This forms the knot. You then bring the needle up where the next knot is wanted, and repeat the operation. *(See illustration of Knot Stitch in Poppy design).* Yellow floss is also used for the stamens (the thread-like portions that run from the centre out to the knots, or anthers), taking but one stitch for each stamen. The veins in the petals are put in in the same way, using a lighter shade of yellow floss, and worked in the same direction as shown by the vein lines in the design. If the work presents a drawn appearance when finished, this can be remedied by steaming the back of it and then stretching it over a board for a short time.

INSTRUCTIONS FOR POPPY DESIGN.

Probably few flowers are more suitable, and as effective for a sofa cushion as the real poppies shown in our study, and illustrated in the finished cushion. These brilliant flowers with their yellowish-green centres and dark brown anthers, when worked upon a copper colored plush, and having olive green plush corners sewn diagonally across two opposite corners, and finished with appropriate silk ball fringe and silk pon-pons for the corners, present a harmonious effect that is very pleasing to the eye.

Let us begin by making a perforated pattern, from the engraving, in the same way as described on page 71. This done, use the French indelible stamping (page 72) in getting the outlines upon the plush. This process takes a little time to dry, but must be thoroughly dry before working. The material is then placed in an embroidery frame. Now make a careful observation of the full size working design and notice how all the stitches are worked, where the needle is first inserted and where brought out; note carefully the *correct slant* that is given to the stem stitch, and the chenille stitch seen in the blossom, and how the knot stitch is made and used in putting in the dark anthers of the poppies. You will require three or four shades of olive green chenille for the stems, leaves and bulbs, and three shades of garnet chenille *(poppy tints)* for the blossoms and buds ; a little yellowish green etching silk for the stamens, a skein of seal brown embroidery silk for the knots with which to put in the anthers, will complete the list of materials. Begin working the stems with the darkest of the three shades of chenille. Commence working the large stem at the bottom, and bring the needle up at the *left-hand side* of the stamped outline : now insert it at the *right-hand* of the outline and bring it out at the left-hand outline, giving it the upward slant shown by the needle in the partly finished stem. Work all the stems first, and then begin the leaves, at the bottom of the spray. These leaves are similar in shape to those of the Scotch Thistle on page 75, and may be worked in the same way, but with olive green shades of chenille. We will begin with the large leaf below the blossom. Thread a large wool needle with your medium shade of olive green chenille and begin working the lower half of the leaf, commencing where the leaf joins the stem. Bring the needle up through the material at the vein, then take it down at the edge of the leaf (giving it the slant indicated by the stitches seen in the engraving). Now bring the needle up again at the *edge* of the leaf, a short distance nearer the point of the leaf. The needle is then taken *down* at the vein of the leaf, and again brought up at the vein, and so on. The finished leaves seen in the engraving show how far apart the stitches should be. Use a lighter shade for the tips of the leaves. When this is done, take a darker shade and work the other half of the leaf. Those parts in the other finished leaves (shown in the engraving) which are intended to be worked in a lighter shade, are shown lighter in the illustration. The other leaves are worked in the same way, varying the shades in each one. The small leaves near the top of the spray are worked in the lighter shades ; so, also, is the small leaf at the bottom.

We will now direct our attention to the bud near the bottom of the spray. It will be seen, by the engraving, that *two short stitches* at the point of the bud are darker than the rest. These *two stitches* are first put in with the darkest shade of *garnet* chenille, and then the rest of the bud is worked with the darkest shade of olive green chenille, bringing the green partly over

the lower ends of the garnet stitches, thus giving the red portion of the bud the appearance of peeping out from under the green. The large blossom may now be worked. Begin at the outside edge of the petal, using the lightest shade of garnet chenille. Work two rows of stitches, of unequal length, around the outside edge of the petal, and also *one* row on each side of the petal where it touches the other petals. Now fill in another row of stitches with the medium shade of chenille, blending the stitches into the lighter shade. The remaining portion near the centre is then filled in with the darkest shade, being very careful to keep the ends of the stitches, which are nearer the centre of the flower, *closer together* than the ends of the stitches nearer the outside edge, so that the petals will converge towards the centre (see finished petal in the large design). That portion of the petal which is shown dark in the engraving indicates the parts that are filled in with the darker shades. The partly finished petal and the one below the finished petal are both worked so as to show a little more *light* garnet chenille near the outside edges, than the finished petal; while the *three* small petals (which are shaded by the green leaves above them) are worked with the darkest shade almost throughout, with the exception of a very few bright stitches at the outside edge of each. The small blossom is worked in the same manner, using only the two lighter shades. In the partly blown flower, the inside portion is all worked with the brightest shade of garnet chenille, with the exception of a few stitches of dark near the top, to indicate the shadow caused by the turning over of the petal. The two outside petals are worked throughout with the darkest shade, with but a few bright stitches at the top of the *outside* upper petal. Now work the upper bud near the large flower. Fill in the top part with the medium shade of chenille, and for that part nearer the bulb use the darkest shade; when this is done, work the bulb (that part of the bud nearer the stem) with the medium shade of olive green chenille, bringing the green chenille up partly on the red portion of the bud.

The bud below this one is worked throughout in olive green, with the exception of two or three stitches of bright garnet chenille at the point. The one above the small blossom shows but one stitch of garnet chenille. Having finished the buds, we will put in the green centres enclosed by the larger circle in each blossom, using the medium shade of olive green chenille, taking the stitches back and forth from the *outside circle* to the small circle.   This done, thread an ordinary needle with seal brown embroidery silk, and put a large knot in the very small inner circle in each flower.   Make smaller knots with the same material for the numerous anthers seen in the engraving, just outside of the larger circle.   The knot stitch is illustrated in the Poppy design. The needle is brought up through the material where the knot is wanted, and the floss is wound twice around the point of the needle ; now insert the needle at the point where it came up (pulling the floss slightly with the left hand), and draw it back through the material.   The knots, stamens and veins are all put in on top of the chenille.   The stamens (thread-like organs) are put in with a yellowish-green etching silk, in single stitches running from the anthers to the centre, as shown in the illustration.

FINISHED SOFA CUSHION, IN POPPY DESIGN.

The veins are put in with dark veining chenille (embroidery floss will do). The direction of the veins and their distance apart is indicated in the worked leaves and in those in outline in the engraving. Your material is now ready to be made up. The plush, upon which the flower is worked, is now cut into the shape shown in the engraved *Sofa Cushion*, and olive green plush is sewed to the two opposite corners, which are shown in the engraved cushion in a lighter tint. Two and a quarter yards of silk ball fringe will be required for trimming, and silk pon-pons for the corners. Fringe and pon-pons of variegated garnet would look pretty

INSTRUCTIONS FOR DESIGN OF FUCHSIAS.

It will be needless to enumerate the number of purposes for which this beautiful design can be used. It would look very pretty painted upon white moleskin velvet and made up into a wall banner, appropriately mounted with brass rod and rings, plush ends and pon-pons. (See colored study on page 63, and directions for painting the Fuchsias). As it furnishes an excellent subject for arrasene work, we will endeavor to make plain the method of operation. It will look very pretty worked on sage green, or old gold colored felt, with plush mountings of a similar shade. Make the pattern and stamp the design upon the felt, according to directions given on page 71. Use the *black liquid stamping*. The stems are worked with a dark green embroidery floss, using such a shade as is seen in the Fuchsia leaves in the colored study, on page 63. The method of working the stems is clearly shown in the illustration. As you near the tops, make the stem stitches longer and narrower. The leaves are worked in three shades of dark green arrasene; thread the arrasene needle with the lightest shade and begin at the outside of the leaf and make an irregular outline stitch, giving the stitches the slant indicated by the stitches shown in the lower half of the partly worked leaf seen in the illustration. Make a row of these stitches on both sides of the upper portion of the leaf. Now fill in the remaining portion with the darker shades, blending the dark stitches into the light ones, nearer the edge. Do not make the light arrasene outline stitches close, so that you can blend the darker stitches into the lighter ones by taking the dark stitches down between the light ones, about half way up the lighter ones.   As you near the top of the spray, use the lighter shades of green.   The flowers may be worked in the same mauve tints seen in the colored study, on page 63, using two shades of mauve arrasene ; or the flowers on one branch may be worked in delicate pink tints, using two or three shades of pink arrasene.

The parts shown light in the finished fuchsia is worked with white arrasene. Fill in a small portion of light mauve arrasene near the white portion, and then work in the darker shade last, as shown in the flower partly worked, blending the stitches into each other.   Vary the shading in each flower.   If it be desired to work the flowers on one branch in pink tints, it can be done in the same way, by using two or three pink shades of arrasene.   It will be found quite a help to refer to the colored study (page 63) while working. The buds are worked with white arrasene, having a very little *pale* green blended in near the bulb *(part near the stem)*.   The bulb is worked with pale green embroidery floss, worked over a yarn foundation, which will give it a rounded appearance.   The yarn foundation is put in on the same principle as the bulb for the Scotch Thistle (page 75), but with finer yarn.   The anthers are put in with the knot stitch, using a bright pink ching silk to make the knots.   The thread-like stamens are put in with bright colored pink etching silk.   The veins are put in the leaves in the following manner :   Thread a common needle with dark green embroidery floss ; bring it up through the material at the *upper end* of the central vein.   Now draw the floss down to the point where *the first cross-vein meets* the central one ; hold the floss into place here with your left thumb ; now insert the needle at the outside end of the first cross-vein, and bring the needle out at the point where it meets the central vein.   But bring the needle out on top of the floss held by your thumb.   Now insert the needle at the outside end of the next vein, on the *other side* of the central vein, and bring it out on top of the thread where this cross-vein meets the central vein ; and so on, till all the veins are put in.   (See veins in the finished leaf and those in outline).

www.ingramcontent.com/pod-product-compliance
Lightning Source LLC
Chambersburg PA
CBHW030538270326
41927CB00008B/1425